THE DARKER SIDE OF LEADERSHIP

Manfred F. R. Kets de Vries is one of the most authoritative voices on organizational development, leadership, executive coaching, and psychotherapy today. In all his roles, he has noticed that questions are now, increasingly, coming back to one thing—the wider state of the world. Using an engaging and highly readable style throughout the book, Manfred helps us to make sense of the confusing and, some might say, psychotic times in which we now live.

Revealing the darker side of leadership, Manfred explores the tendency for people to adopt "sheeple" or herd-like behavior, the populist threats that we are facing, the dangers that come with feelings of perceived injustice, the rise of dictatorships, the impact of Leviathan (neo-authoritarian) leadership behavior, and the psychological impact of wars. Guided by various theoretical concepts, the book provides readers with a better understanding of the underlying forces that drive these phenomena to the surface. What are the psychological dynamics at play? Why do groups of people behave in this manner? Beyond merely diagnosing what's happening, Manfred introduces various coping strategies to counteract the emergence of these regressive forces.

The book offers a unique and original approach to answering the micro- and macro-psychological questions of how to mitigate against populism and autocratic leadership and will be of interest to the general reader as well as the key audiences of organizational leaders, psychoanalysts, coaches, psychotherapists, sociologists, and social psychologists.

Manfred F. R. Kets de Vries is the Distinguished Clinical Professor of Leadership Development and Organizational Change at INSEAD and the Founder of INSEAD's Global Leadership Center. *The Financial Times, Wirtschaftswoche, Le Capital, El Pais,* and *The Economist* have rated him among the world's leading management thinkers. He is the author of more than 50 books and hundreds of articles, and the recipient of numerous awards, including four honorary doctorates.

THE DARKER SIDE OF LEADERSHIP

Pythons Devouring Crocodiles

Manfred F. R. Kets de Vries

Routledge
Taylor & Francis Group

LONDON AND NEW YORK

Cover image: Philip Harris

First published 2024
by Routledge
4 Park Square, Milton Park, Abingdon, Oxon OX14 4RN

and by Routledge
605 Third Avenue, New York, NY 10158

Routledge is an imprint of the Taylor & Francis Group, an informa business

British Library Cataloguing-in-Publication Data
A catalogue record for this book is available from the British Library

Library of Congress Cataloging-in-Publication Data
Names: Kets de Vries, Manfred F. R., author.
Title: The darker side of leadership : pythons devouring crocodiles / Manfred F. R. Kets de Vries.
Description: Abingdon, Oxon ; New York, NY : Routledge, 2024. | Includes bibliographical references and index.
Identifiers: LCCN 2023052444 (print) | LCCN 2023052445 (ebook) | ISBN 9781032731858 (hardback) | ISBN 9781032705200 (paperback) | ISBN 9781003427117 (ebook)
Subjects: LCSH: Leadership.
Classification: LCC BF637.L4 K457 2024 (print) | LCC BF637.L4 (ebook) | DDC 158.4—dc23/eng/20231204
LC record available at https://lccn.loc.gov/2023052444
LC ebook record available at https://lccn.loc.gov/2023052445

ISBN: 978-1-032-73185-8 (hbk)
ISBN: 978-1-032-70520-0 (pbk)
ISBN: 978-1-003-42711-7 (ebk)

DOI: 10.4324/9781003427117

Typeset in Garamond
by Apex CoVantage, LLC

CONTENTS

ABOUT THE AUTHOR

Manfred F. R. Kets de Vries brings a different view to the much-studied subjects of organizational dynamics, leadership, executive coaching, and psychotherapy. Bringing to bear his knowledge and experience of economics (Econ. Drs., University of Amsterdam), management (ITP, MBA, and DBA, Harvard Business School), and psychoanalysis (Membership Canadian Psychoanalytic Society, Paris Psychoanalytic Society, and the International Psychoanalytic Association), he explores individual and societal existential dilemmas in depth.

The Distinguished Clinical Professor of Leadership Development and Organizational Change at INSEAD, he is the Founder of INSEAD's Executive Master Program in Change Management. He has been a pioneer in team coaching as an intervention method to help organizations and people change. As an educator, he has received INSEAD's distinguished MBA teacher award six times. He has held professorships at McGill University, the École des Hautes Études Commerciales, Montreal, and the Harvard Business School. He is also a distinguished visiting professor at the European School for Management and Technology (ESMT), Berlin. He has lectured at management institutions around the world. *The Financial Times, Le Capital, Wirtschaftswoche,* and *The Economist* have rated Kets de Vries among the world's leading management thinkers and among the most influential contributors to human resource management.

Kets de Vries is the author, co-author, or editor of more than 50 books, including *The Neurotic Organization, Power and the Corporate Mind, Organizational Paradoxes, Struggling with the Demon: Perspectives on Individual and Organizational Irrationality, Handbook of Character Studies, The Irrational Executive, Leaders, Fools and Impostors, Life and Death in the Executive Fast Lane, Prisoners of Leadership, The Leadership Mystique, The Happiness Equation, Are Leaders Made or Are They Born? The Case of Alexander the Great, The New Russian Business Elite, Leadership by Terror: Finding Shaka Zulu in the Attic, The Leader on the Couch, Coach and Couch, The Family Business on the Couch, Sex, Money, Happiness, and Death: The Quest for Authenticity, Reflections on Leadership and Character, Reflections on Leadership and Career, Reflections on Organizations, The Coaching Kaleidoscope, The Hedgehog Effect: The Secrets of High Performance Teams, Mindful Leadership Coaching: Journeys into the Interior, You Will Meet a Tall Dark Stranger: Executive Coaching Challenges, Telling Fairy Tales in the Boardroom: How to Make Sure Your Organization Lives Happily Ever After, Riding the Leadership Roller Coaster: A Psychological Observer's Guide, Down the Rabbit Hole of Leadership: Leadership Pathology of Everyday Life, The CEO Whisperer: Meditations on Leaders, Life and Change, Quo Vadis: The Existential Challenges of Leaders, Leadership Unhinged: Essays on the Ugly, the Bad, and the Weird, Leading Wisely: Becoming a Reflective Leader in Turbulent Times, The Daily Perils of Executive Life: How to Survive When Dancing on Quicksand, The Path to Authentic Leadership: Dancing with the Ouroboros,* and *A Life Well Lived: Dialogues with a Kabouter.* Furthermore, he has designed a number of 360-degree feedback instruments, including the widely used *Global Executive Leadership Mirror, Global Executive Leadership Inventory,* and the *Organizational Culture Audit.*

In addition, Kets de Vries has published more than 400 academic papers as chapters in books and as articles. He has also written more than 100 case studies, including seven that received the Best Case of the Year award. He has written hundreds of mini-articles (blogs) for the *Harvard Business Review, INSEAD Knowledge,* and other digital outlets. He is also a regular writer for various other magazines. His work has been featured in such publications as *The New York Times, The Wall Street Journal, The Los Angeles Times, Fortune, Business Week, The Economist, The Financial Times, The Straits Times, The New Statesman, The Harvard Business Review, Le Figaro, El Pais,* and *Het Financieele Dagblad.* His books and articles have been translated into more than 30 languages.

Furthermore, Kets de Vries is a member of 17 editorial boards and is a Fellow of the Academy of Management. In addition, he is on the board of a number of charitable organizations. He is also a founding member of the International Society for the Psychoanalytic Study of Organizations (ISPSO), which has honored him as a lifetime member. Kets de Vries is also the first non-US recipient of the International Leadership Association Lifetime Achievement Award for his contributions to leadership research and development. In addition, he has received a Lifetime Achievement Award from Germany for his advancement of executive education. The American Psychological Association has honored him with the "Harry and Miriam Levinson Award" for his contributions to Organizational Consultation. He is also the recipient of the "Freud Memorial Award" for his work to further the interface between management and psychoanalysis. In addition, he has also received the "Vision of Excellence Award" from the Harvard Institute of Coaching. Kets de Vries is the first beneficiary of INSEAD's Dominique Héau Award for "Inspiring Educational Excellence." Furthermore, he has been honored with four honorary doctorates. The Dutch government has made him an Officer in the Order of Oranje Nassau.

Kets de Vries works as a consultant on organizational design/ transformation and strategic human resource management for companies worldwide. As an educator and consultant, he has worked in more than 40 countries. In his role as a consultant, he is also the founder-chairman of the Kets de Vries Institute (KDVI), a boutique global strategic leadership development consulting firm with associates worldwide (www.kdvi.com).

On a very different note, Kets de Vries has also been the first fly fisherman in Outer Mongolia (at the time, becoming the world record holder of the Siberian hucho taimen trout). He is a member of New York's Explorers Club. In his spare time, he can be found in the rainforests or savannas of Central and Southern Africa, the Siberian taiga, the Ussuri Krai, Kamchatka, the Pamir Mountains, the Altai Mountains, Arnhemland, or within the Arctic Circle.

E-mail: manfred.ketsdevries@insead.edu
Website: www.kdvi.com

INTRODUCTION

The whole world is divided for me into two parts: one is she, and there is all happiness, hope, light; the other is where she is not, and there is dejection and darkness.

—Leo Tolstoy

We live in an age which is so possessed by demons, that soon we shall only be able to do goodness and justice in the deepest secrecy, as if it were a crime.

—Franz Kafka

The stimulus for writing this book of essays has been Russia's devastating invasion of Ukraine. Due to my interest in Russian literature, I have always been a Russophile, but the "special military operation," more aptly described as a war, has made this *affaire du coeur* hard to maintain. Interestingly enough, when the war broke out, I was directing a leadership seminar in Moscow for a group of senior executives. The members of the seminar were struck with disbelief on hearing news of the invasion and dispersed,

DOI: 10.4324/9781003427117-1

most likely to figure out how to go on with their lives. They were undoubtedly talking to their loved ones while also assessing the temperature in their organizations, trying to think through their options. Later I learned that many of them had left the country, some of them went almost bankrupt, while others still struggle to make sense of it all.

As a person who was born during World War II, this "special military operation" evoked many dark associations for me. Growing up after the war, my brother and I were constantly exposed to my mother's accounts of the terrible things that transpired in the Netherlands, my country of birth. Later, I would learn that a large number of my family members had fallen victim to the Nazis' atrocities during that period. I also vividly recall eagerly turning on the radio as a child, joining my maternal grandfather to listen to the proceedings of the Nuremberg trials, where the Nazi war criminals were being judged. Those radio programs left a deep impression on me. Nowadays, thinking of the atrocities that happened during World War II, I often reflect on the famous quote by Greek historian Herodotus, "In peace, sons bury their fathers. In war, fathers bury their sons." All too often, it appears that older men declare war so that younger men can die. How pointless wars can be.

I could have flown out of Moscow the same day the war started, but I was curious to observe how the Russian people would react to this event. As I had made a number of appointments, I thought that these meetings would give me the opportunity to discuss the matter with a diverse group of people. That evening, while en route to a dinner engagement, I witnessed the police beating up anti-war protesters. Later, during dinner, my guest—an ex-student—relayed the reason for his depressed mood: not only had his company been sanctioned, his wife and his daughter were currently in Kiev, and, given the situation, he was wondering how to get them out. That was the beginning of a series of strange encounters to follow in those first confusing days of war.

I was also curious about the kind of news presented on Russian television. As I listened to some of the discussions surrounding the war, it felt as if I were living in an alternative universe, psychotic-like in environment, a surreal world of conspiracy theories. The main theme of these televised discussions was the notion of a malevolent West trying to subjugate Russia. Considering previous failed attempts by other nations to conquer Russia, I found this idea bizarre. Meanwhile, according to the television commentators, Russia was heroically fighting against neo-Nazis and Ukrainian satanists, all in the name of upholding traditional values. In reality, however, Russia's leaders were attempting to justify what was essentially an old-fashioned colonial war driven by imperialistic ambitions.

The craziness of it all, combined with my interest in the darker side of leadership, led me to write these essays. While my usual writings tend towards a micro-psychological nature, in this case I decided to take a somewhat different tack, more of a macro-psychological approach could make sense of the shadowy side of popular movements. It became clear, however, that this "special military operation" exemplified once again how easily regression can occur not only at an individual level but also on a massive, national scale. It was evident that war can serve as the ideal catalyst for the rise of demagogue-like leadership. All that I witnessed in those first days had a distinctly Kafkaesque quality.

Franz Kafka has always been one of my favorite authors. Therefore, it is not surprising that I was reminded of his dark view of humanity while in Moscow at the onset of the war. The unfolding events served as a stark reminder that the writings of Kafka have a Promethean quality. Like Prometheus, the god of forethought, Kafka appeared to anticipate the terrible events that were to come like a prophet of another time.

Of course, Kafka's bizarre and sometimes surreal writings must be understood in the context of the disintegration of the Austro-Hungarian Empire, a development that led to World War I—an atrocity immense enough to determine the whole course of the 20th century. In hindsight, Kafka appears to have understood something profound before most others even began to grasp its significance. His generation and the one that followed would become victims of history, succumbing to the destructive forces they faced.

Kafka recognized unequivocally that the rise of populist, demagogue-like leaders—more popularly named dictators—had the power to thrust us into a world with an oppressive, nightmarish, and illogical quality. It would be a world where people were crushed by nonsensical, blind authority. Evil and sinister powers would maintain control, fostering an atmosphere of systematic oppression. In this surreal new world, alienated and anguished individuals would try to transcend their fate, pursuing unattainable goals, only to find their efforts were in vain. Facing incomprehensible authority figures, a sense of helplessness and hopelessness would prevail. This Kafkaesque world would demand great resilience, as escape from its clutches would be impossible. No matter how ardently Kafka's protagonists tried to escape the forces they faced, they would only find themselves sinking deeper into the quagmire of authority. In this Kafkaesque world, the perpetually demoralized common people would be forever seeking justice, only to be met with an administrative apparatus intentionally designed to confine them within an inescapable maze.

The absurd and sinister totalitarianism found in Kafka's stories finds echoes in countries like the former Soviet Union, present-day Russia, North Korea, China, Iran, Eritrea, Myanmar, or Venezuela. These nations are characterized by a callous dismissal of human and constitutional rights, where the lives of individual citizens go unvalued. In these countries we witness severe abuses of power, disdain for legal procedures, and the perversion of justice. They exhibit a multi-layered, hierarchical world, divided between the haves and have-nots, the bourgeoisie and the proletariat, the powerful and the powerless. Instead of guiding and guarding its citizens, the legal systems in these countries force citizens to crawl through a web of cold, corrupt, bureaucratized systems. People may be arrested, punished, or even executed without being given any justification. Authority appears inaccessible and anonymous, imprisonment is unfounded and baseless, and justice lies forever out of reach. In this respect, Kafka's stories shed light on the illusion that the law is open and accessible to everyone, exposing the indifference and insensitivity of those in power. Furthermore, it portrays the futile struggle of the general population against a government that remains deliberately distant from the very people it is supposed to serve.

I strongly believe that Kafka's stories should be regarded as a warning of what can happen when human rights are no longer respected. Unfortunately, Kafka's stories present a world far closer to reality than we dare to imagine. He intuited the regressive tendencies within human nature better than anybody else. In a similar sense, Putin's "special military operation" instilled a sense of foreboding within me as individuals once again became victims of its relentless march.

It is with these terrifying thoughts in mind that I wrote these chapters. They explore themes such as the psychotic world we live in, the tendency for people to adopt sheeple or herd-like behavior, and the dangers that come with feelings of perceived injustice; they highlight the insidious nature of dictatorships, the impact of the Leviathan (neo-authoritarian) leadership behavior, and the psychology of war and its aftermath. Drawing upon my training as a psychoanalyst, student of organizations and leadership scholar, I look at these phenomena from a psychodynamic-systemic perspective. However, when appropriate, I also apply ideas from developmental psychology, evolutionary theory, anthropology, sociology, and neurology. Guided by theoretical concepts derived from these fields of study, I aim to provide readers with a better understanding of the underlying forces that drive these phenomena to the surface. What are the psychological dynamics at play? Why do groups of people behave in this manner? But beyond merely diagnosing what's happening, I also introduce various possible coping strategies to counteract the emergence of these regressive forces. My ultimate objective is to prevent the rise of demagogue-like leaders. I hope that by exploring issues so intrinsic to war and peace, readers will gain greater insight into why people descend into such self-created nightmares. Most importantly, I hope that a greater understanding of the various psychological processes involved will enable us to steer clear of these all-too-human patterns of regressive behavior.

Not very far from where I live in Paris is the famous Institute Curie, named after Pierre and Marie Curie. Marie Salomea Skłodowska–Curie, a Polish and naturalized French physicist, became the first woman to receive the Nobel Prize and remains the only woman to have received the prize twice. Beyond her scientific achievements, Marie Curie exemplified a belief in the future of humankind. Certainly, her perspective on world affairs differs greatly from that of Franz Kafka, once stating:

> You cannot hope to build a better world without improving the individuals. To that end, each of us must work for his own improvement and, at the same time, share a general responsibility for all humanity, our particular duty being to aid those to whom we think we can be most useful.

Thus, despite the dark nature of these essays, it is my sincere hope that many people will heed her profound words.

1

LIVING IN A PSYCHOTIC AGE

The masses have never thirsted after truth. They turn aside from evidence that is not to their taste, preferring to deify error, if error seduce them. Whoever can supply them with illusions is easily their master; whoever attempts to destroy their illusions is always their victim. An individual in a crowd is a grain of sand amid other grains of sand, which the wind stirs up at will.

—Gustave Le Bon

A SMALL WALK

As I was walking down my street in Paris, at the corner of Place Saint-Michel, I noticed an individual carrying a sign that read: "Behold, the End is Near." I must admit that I first found this statement rather naive. However, upon reflecting on the current state of the world, I realized there could be some truth in those words. It is evident that humanity isn't in good health. Our world is one of conflict and stress and strife. The apocalyptic horsemen seem to be everywhere, manifested in the forms of

DOI: 10.4324/9781003427117-2

war, terrorism, nuclear threat, global warming, starvation, migration, great income inequalities, pandemics of illness like Covid-19, and—perhaps most insidious to society and most relevant to these essays—the repeated emergence of toxic leaders on the world stage.

PSYCHIC EPIDEMICS

Stress can do strange things to us. It affects our minds, causing us to view situations in bizarre and distorted ways. The psychoanalyst Carl Jung once stated that the greatest threat to civilization does not lie with the forces of nature or any physical disease but rather with our inability to deal with the forces of our own psyche. To quote him directly:

> It is not famine, not earthquakes, not microbes, not cancer but man himself who is man's greatest danger to man, for the simple reason that there is no adequate protection against psychic epidemics, which are infinitely more devastating than the worst of natural catastrophes.[1]

Homo sapiens are herd animals that are susceptible to falling prey to strange psychic epidemics or forms of mass madness when under significant stress. As a result, large numbers of people may lose touch with reality and descend into a delusionary state. The potential consequences can be catastrophic.

Jung used the term "psychic epidemic" to describe this phenomenon, but other terms have been used to refer to these strange social events. Examples include "mass psychogenic disorder," "epidemic hysteria," "mass hysteria," "mass delusion," "collective obsessions," "*folie en masse*" (mass insanity) and "mass psychoses." These collective phenomena apply to a multitude of crazes, panics, and abnormal group beliefs. However, many of the names given to these mass delusions are not particularly specific. In fact, the wide range of phenomena that fall under Jung's description of "psychic epidemic" suggests that the term has become somewhat of a catch-all, applicable to anything with negative connotations involving the participation of large groups of people. Strange social forces seem to be at work, contributing to and encouraging abnormal belief systems and behavioral patterns. In fact, if creatures from outer space were to observe the many existing conspiratorial belief systems and pseudoscientific outlooks, they would declare their advocates delusional.

Given the nature of these mass delusions, the term "psychosis" may be more appropriate. Essentially, an individual experiencing a psychotic episode is no longer able to share the same consensual reality as those around them. Classic symptoms include sensory hallucinations, fixed delusions, false beliefs, absolutist thinking, and paranoid ideation. People who suffer from psychosis live in a very strange world, with thought processes or perceptions of events that appear alien to others. Their impaired sense of reality results in them struggling to differentiate between what is real and what is not. Psychotics often feel completely lost. The world they live in no longer makes any sense; their means of coping is to create a parallel fantasy world that makes sense to them, however bizarre it might appear to others.

GUIDING MYTHS

It seems that these individuals have lost the guiding myths and sense of direction by which they once lived. However, in contemporary society, where the aforementioned "horsemen" are prevalent, we need myths to live by. As social creatures, human beings have always sought collective unifying principles. Subscribing to these unifying myths allows them to reinforce their beliefs and justify their actions. Guiding myths help them understand the notions of fate and destiny and provide symbols, language, and expressive ways to cope with the challenges of life. In their search for meaning, people need stories to help cope with and conquer the unknown. And they are always seeking out stories that provide guidance on where they came from, where they are, and where they are going.

From a cultural-historical perspective, human civilization has been built on various central guiding myths. For instance, in the Western world, Christianity provided guidance for everyday life for thousands of years. After the Renaissance, rationalism became a central guiding myth. Modernity brought about a belief that technology could and would change the lives of humans for the better. However, in our current digital age, there appears to be a lack of such fundamental guiding myths that help individuals make sense of their existence. This absence of general guidance and unity may encourage individual psychotic behavior to turn into mass psychotic behavior.

THE ENTRY OF MASS PSYCHOSIS

Very little is needed for individual delusionary thoughts to spread and become pervasive among large groups of people, distorting their sense of reality. Much like individuals with psychosis struggle to make sense of an incomprehensible world, groups of people might cling to delusional beliefs as a coping mechanism for what they perceive to be a terrifying environment. Often, real or imagined threats augment their distressed mental state. Accepting bizarre ideas becomes a way to manage floods of negative emotion, to feel sane in a seemingly insane world. It can be seen as a convoluted attempt to reorder their inner world and attain a sense of inner security. In their pursuit of meaning, these people will grasp at even the most nonsensical of straws, and over time these delusions turn into pathological responses to what they perceive to be danger.

Examples of mass psychosis are diverse, ranging from the bizarre Children's Crusade and the dancing mania of the Middle Ages to the Salem Witch trials in colonial Massachusetts, the strange tulip mania in Holland, the Tanganyika laughter epidemic in Tanzania, and the Havana Syndrome in Cuba. Unusual social phenomena can also include peculiar obsessions, fashion fads, and participation in raves. Frequently, natural disasters or events serve as psychogenic triggers for the more disturbing historical examples of social madness. For example, in the Middle Ages, the black death (bubonic plague) was a major trigger. Historically, outbreaks of social madness often occurred within close-knit social groups that were united by strong religious beliefs.

One of the most disconcerting examples of mass psychosis in the past two centuries has been totalitarian and ideological experiments. These peculiar forms of mass psychosis are perhaps one of the greatest threats to humanity. In these instances, the centralization of state power comes at the expense of individual rights and has been seen to result in tremendous suffering, as well as a dramatic negative economic impact. For example, ideology and pathology have resulted in the death of tens of millions of people in the Soviet Union, Nazi Germany, North Korea, China, and Cambodia. These dreadful examples are characterized by a collective detachment from reality, primarily involving people who have resorted to delusional thinking, fear, and paranoia. And when mass psychosis takes hold, common human decency tends to fall by the wayside. Citizens of a country will live in a permanent state of terror, surrounded by perceived internal and external "enemies." Consequently, people start to "eat" their own, finding ways to eliminate those who they deem to be non-believers.

These forms of mass psychosis demonstrate that we are not necessarily in control of our minds, even if we'd like to believe we are. We are strongly influenced by what is happening around us and constantly bombarded by external forces, sometimes without being conscious of them. This makes humans both vulnerable and gullible, especially when triggered by social stress. After all, fear and anxiety foster an ideal breeding ground for outbreaks of unusual and uncharacteristic beliefs and behaviors. Interestingly, these strange beliefs and behavioral patterns are frequently associated with social issues and scientific matters that have become politicized, resulting in complex conspiracy theories. In an age of uncertainty, these factors are likely to distort our sense of reality and impede our critical thinking.

SOCIAL CONTAGION

Generally speaking, a sense of alienation, disorientation, and fear creates ideal conditions for strange ideas to take root. In the constant search for certainty and meaning, driven by the inherent human fear of death and the unknown, individuals develop abnormal sets of ideas and beliefs. Despite their irrationality, however, humans are social creatures who crave connection and communication with others. This results in such ideas becoming contagious and for a localized situation or belief to gradually evolve into a case of mass psychosis.

Through interaction with others, these strange ideas—often focused on all that is wrong with society—engender social pressure and groupthink. Persuasive and charismatic leaders increase the likelihood of groupthink, inspiring people in uniquely charismatic ways to agree with their opinions. On the whole, the more people that hold similar beliefs, the more they consciously or unconsciously exert social pressure on others to conform.

FOLLOWING THE HERD

Group settings typically inspire theatrics and situations in which the compulsion to conform can be hard to resist. Mass meetings in particular can have a hypnotic effect on those present. A persuasive leader can be extremely intimidating, putting enormous pressure on individuals in large groups to think alike. These dynamics harness the innate human desire to fit in and create the ideal environment for people to abandon or censor their own opinions, beliefs, and even thoughts. Without conscious awareness, people lose their sense of individuality and feed off one another's emotional reactions, resulting in an escalation of their concerns.

When enough people accept delusional ideas, large sections of society lose touch with reality and construct a parallel, psychotic-like universe with an unscrupulous blend of fact and fiction. They combine real events with imaginary ones—a pathological approach to instill order in their lives and explain their bizarre beliefs and behavior. While it may seem like they have found a convoluted way to escape their fears, it comes at a great cost.

A WORLD OF CONSPIRACIES

People who fall under the spell of mass psychosis often find themselves living in a world full of conspiracies. They believe that enemies are ubiquitous and threatening, and their life is characterized by a pervasive atmosphere of terror. Although this worldview is delusional, paranoid individuals perceive a degree of truth in their thoughts and don't realize that they're behaving in an unusual manner. What is even more disturbing, however, is the likely decline in moral values and civility. Gradually, they become increasingly irrational, irresponsible, emotionally unstable, and unreliable. In some cases, this may even lead to forms of violent behavior that they would not have even considered otherwise. Unfortunately, such negative and destructive behavior is contagious, particularly in large groups. And this is the ideal time for a demagogue-like leader to emerge and turn people on each other by exploiting their fears—their belief that "the enemy" is in their midst.

Former US President Donald Trump exemplifies exactly this paranoid thought process in his conviction that conspirators lurk in every corner. His disturbing antics show that his beliefs have become self-fulfilling prophecies. Despite evidence to the contrary, he will claim that the presidential election had been stolen from him. In addition, many of his followers, goaded by Trump's interest in pseudo-science, still believe that the Covid-19 vaccine was a government tool for thought control or that QAnon is a reliable source of information. Unfortunately, he is not the only political leader in a position of influence propagating such ideas. Brazilian ex-President Jair Bolsonaro, for example, also appears to live in a world of conspiracies. He also promoted the notion of a vast leftist conspiracy that stole the presidential election from him. Does that sound familiar?

Globally, however, Russia's Vladimir Putin remains the most dangerous conspiracy monger of modern times, especially given his country's vast nuclear arsenal. Like many other world leaders, he lives in a paranoid world, effectively circulating the idea among his citizens that the West is intent on obliterating Russia. He also claims that the Western world has abandoned religion and embraced satanism—bizarre ideas that have been shared and accepted by many Russian citizens. Given this paranoid outlook, it is no wonder that he is making threats about possible nuclear strikes. Unfortunately, the very nature of conspiracy theories is that they are nearly impossible to disprove. When presented with facts to the contrary, those adopting the same paranoid worldview find ways to weave new evidence into their conspiracy theories.

HYPER-INDIVIDUALISM

The development of paranoid thinking can be seen as a search for certainty and a sense of purpose in a highly uncertain, anxiety-inducing world. We could go even as far as to reframe this phenomenon as a sane response to an insane society. The reality is that these emotions are the result of people feeling disconnected and lacking a sense of community. In the past, people lived in smaller communities and were more likely to develop closer personal relationships, a strong sense of common identity, and shared values and norms. In our digital age, however, these pillars of security have all but disappeared. Individualism and technological infrastructure have fostered a culture of isolation, resulting in people having limited physical interaction with their fellow citizens.

The recent pandemic exacerbated the situation by forcing people to shift all activity into their private sphere. As a result, public engagement and communal attachment fell even further by the wayside. Social media platforms such as Facebook, Instagram, Snapchat, TikTok, WhatsApp, Telegram, YouTube, Pinterest, and Twitter have prevailed and, in many cases, reduced or replaced previous forms of physical social interaction. While the worst ramifications of the pandemic have subsided, many people still live in disturbing isolation. Consequently, hyper-individualism has become the main construct in the narrative of Western society, eclipsing communities, family, religion, or citizenship. Such an outlook also nurtures highly narcissistic behavior.

These recent developments have granted amateurs the authority typically attributed to experts. Many leaders have gained power due to superficial popularity contests, and expertise has devalued as a currency, both in politics and society at large. The absence of local, personal forms of fellowship and solidarity explains why people are more likely to be attracted to cults of personality and identity politics. Nowadays, expertise and knowledge are no longer necessary for political success; popularity and showmanship can masquerade as administrative competence. Ironically, these advances in individualism have contributed to conformism, submission, and mind control.

THE RISE OF THE DEMAGOGUE

Simplistic populist movements, driven by power-hungry, demagogue-like leaders represent the greatest mortal threat to liberal democracies. Such leaders, once in positions of power and authority, often externalize their conspiracy-prone outlook and seize the opportunity to act it out on a public stage. Isolated and anxious individuals are more susceptible to these thought patterns, which makes for a willing audience. After all, isolation has always been an ideal breeding ground for paranoid thinking. When stress becomes toxic enough to harm well-being at an individual and collective level, it can lead to a psychic epidemic.

Invariably, the first to suffer from mass psychosis are the most vulnerable individuals, as evidenced by the cult-like followers of Trump. Periods of great uncertainty have always presented opportunities for autocrats and despots to seduce such people. In fact, demagogues consistently thrive in conditions of fear. When people feel helpless and scared, they become more impressionable and prone to regressive behavior. Demagogues recognize this as an opportunity for their skilled and seductive campaigns, taking advantage of people's vulnerable mental states.

TRANSFERENCE PROCESSES

Demagogue-like leaders clearly know how to hypnotize and seduce their audience by creating symbiotic relationships. Psychoanalysts would interpret this strange psychological connection as transference processes (idealizing and mirroring) gone wrong. Idealizing and mirroring transference reactions involves taking cues and behaviors from others and unconsciously attributing them to other people's emotions, attitudes, or desires that originate from childhood. In other words, people redirect feelings or desires that are associated with important figures in their life to a new person.

In the context of leadership dynamics, these transferential processes of mirroring and idealizing become crucial. "Mirror-hungry" people often suffer from feelings of worthlessness, which can stem from a lack of recognition during critical developmental phases of their childhood. Hence, they may have profound insecurities, constantly search for confirmation and recognition of their worth, and feel compelled to be in the limelight. In contrast, "ideal-hungry" people—who may also have experienced disillusionment during childhood—seek to fill an internal void by attaching themselves to idealized figures. For them, idealizing becomes a way of coping with feelings of helplessness. They deify people of importance to them and hope that by supporting the same beliefs they will acquire some of their power and worth.[2]

This dynamic between leader and followers can develop into a collusive relationship. Leaders who are hungry for adulation project a grandiose image, while their followers yearn for a parental figure to protect and take care of them. The "great leader" thus becomes a figure of fascination, deified by followers who are only too willing to see what they want to see. In short, they become victims of a mass delusion. These followers regress to a child-like, dependency state, and leaders find the affirmation hard to resist.

This interplay turns into a mutual appreciation society, a symbiotic bond that encourages leaders to act in ways that shore up their image rather than serve the needs of their constituency. This kind of interdependency is an open invitation for power-drunk leaders who encourage followers to forsake reality and allow past hopes and fantasies to govern their interactions. This symbiosis can turn rapidly into a cult-like relationship with the danger of descending into mass psychosis within reach. Trump's MAGA ideological movement is just one tragic illustration.

REGRESSIVE BEHAVIOR

What we can observe is how leaders who are psychologically unstable reject any realities that do not align with their distorted worldview.

In an alarmingly short space of time their contagious pathology may spread to their followers. These leaders may gain complete control over their followers' lives by preying on their ignorance, in turn cultivating an obedient and submissive following. Evidently, the combination of deified leadership and a dependent population will not be conducive to a progressive society. A more likely outcome will be one of regression, leading to primitive kinds of behavior that, under normal circumstances, would be unimaginable.

In these situations, instinctual defense mechanisms such as splitting and projection will become prevalent. As master manipulators, these leaders will project feelings of injury, anger, and hatred onto individuals or groups who they perceive to be non-believers. Being a member of the in-group means sharing the leader's projections, and those unwilling to accept their point of view will be vilified, persecuted, and, in the worst cases, even imprisoned or killed. Such actions contribute to a pervasive climate of fear and anxiety, which only allows these leaders to maintain and strengthen their powerbase.

Given their position and authority, demagogue-like leaders can easily spread their distorted perspectives through a population, creating delusional experiences and paranoia in previously rational individuals. However, like members of a cult, their followers are unable to see the harm being done and don't realize that their blind loyalty may lead to suffering or even social ruin on a mass scale.

To secure dependency, these leaders will also play on their followers' sense of perceived victimhood. They will repeatedly emphasize how out-groups (the "enemies") have taken advantage of them, that they have been wronged, and that life hasn't been fair to them. Demagogue-like leaders know that deceiving people in such a way will prevent them from seeing the truth. Regrettably, their followers will be unaware of their descent into collective madness.

THE ROLE OF MASS MEDIA

Toxic leaders retain control over their followers through controlled media coverage that spreads misinformation and distorts existing threats and crises. As part of this negative propaganda, they rely on either fake news or a skillful blend of fact and fiction. Sowing confusion allows them to maintain a regressed populace and keep people off their guard.

Additionally, demagogue leaders recognize the value of constant repetition. A lie repeated many times becomes more believable and entrancing. Regularly repeated nonsense—such as the "Stop the steal" or "Lock her up" slogans used by Trump—can have a greater impact than logical thinking when it comes to influencing the masses. Digital technology has only provided a more direct way to provoke mass psychosis. With the power of social media, it is now even easier to override rational thinking and to infect people's minds. The ability of these leaders to manipulate collective emotion is precisely what makes them so perilous.

It is clear that in countries such as North Korea, Myanmar, Iran, or even Russia, isolating populations and restricting access to information have encouraged the disintegration of normal social interaction. Isolating people has always been an effective way to encourage abnormal thought patterns, obedience, and submissiveness. It explains why the leaders of these countries go to great lengths to block normal social interactions and prevent their constituency from adopting a more reflective stand.

BREAKING THE SPELL

English novelist Rudyard Kipling famously pointed out how extremely challenging it is to "keep your head when all about you are losing theirs." It is near impossible to resist the pull of a mass psychosis when everyone else is under its spell. Power-hungry leaders feed off mass contagion as they rise to power, leading to autocratic or even despotic rule. A population's susceptibility to psychological contagion is why democracy will always be a fragile creation. Under totalitarian regimes, the spontaneity and creativity that drive a society forward are lost, resulting in stagnation, destruction, and death.

When autocracy or despotism is the order of the day, people rapidly lose their sense of self and become embroiled in backward thought processes that rob them of their dignity. The Latin proverb *homo homini lupus*, or "man is wolf to man," becomes all too true. People become predatory, cruel, and behave more like animals than civilized human beings. Bizarre, ideological thoughts triumph over rationality and logical thinking. In fact, those who hold onto delusional narratives tend to bulldoze over reality in their attempts to deny that their own narrative may be false. Consequently, measures must be taken to prevent the rise of mass psychosis.

THE NEED FOR "EMOTIONAL JUDO"

Immunizing individuals against mass seduction will always be an uphill struggle. Many find it easier to remain in a socially vegetative state and let others do the thinking. However, this mindset can lead people to resemble members of a cult or victims of abuse. They become emotionally bonded to the cult leader or abuser and are unable to see the harm being done to them. When individuals are under such control, it is no longer possible to appeal to logic or reason with them. The presentation of facts is not enough to dislodge their beliefs—they need to deal with the underlying emotions, opinions, facts, and counterarguments.

Changing the minds of these individuals and emboldening them to doubt the validity of their beliefs requires a form of "emotional judo." The idea is to move with, and not against, the opponent to break down their defenses. It is necessary to have them explore the consequences of their behavior and make them aware of what will happen if they continue to follow the path that they're on. Counterarguments need to be introduced subtly, as direct disagreement or pointing out their errors will only raise their defenses. Realistic information, contrary to the false information they have been fed, should be innocuously included in discussions to weaken their resistance. Humor can also be highly effective in counterbalancing whatever propaganda they have consumed. However, it is crucial that those trying to change minds secure and safeguard their own mental health, given what they're up against.

THE EXIT OF THE LEADER

An important step in disabling mass psychosis is to remove demagogue leaders from positions of power and influence. While their departure may be the most direct form of healing, it is not sufficient in itself to break the spell. People need to be re-educated in order to understand why they were deceived and to prevent a recurrence. Often, this is a result of their own psychological defense against pain and disappointment or a need to falsify reality. Thus, more needs to be done to avoid the emergence of another pathological figure enticing vulnerable people with yet another "quick fix" solution to their problems. It is critical to change the circumstances that led to these distorted beliefs in the first place.

REMOVING THE HURTS

In attempting to break the spell cast by these leaders, it is worth questioning how far a follower's sense of being wronged may have any roots in reality. If people are disenfranchised or suffering, financially or otherwise, they are more likely to be lured by the siren song of demagogues. As we know, strange ideologies and conspiracy theories are more attractive to those in distress. Therefore, it is vital to change the circumstances that contributed to their flawed belief systems. Reducing any form of inequality, whether economic, racial, or gender related, can help greatly in preventing mass psychotic ideas coming to the fore and growing more extreme.

MEDIA MANAGEMENT

As it stands, the social media business model is one driven by controversy, fear, negativity, divisiveness, and disinformation. Owners of these media businesses capitalize on this—their algorithms attract extremists and prioritize "engagement," which often means pushing inflammatory, tribalizing, or conspiratorial content. Regrettably, our mental conditioning leads us to over-focus on situations involving misery and catastrophe. Thus, social media algorithms are designed to trigger our dopamine neural circuits, which release a chemical messenger that provides waves of satisfaction. It is this neurological process that attracts us to bad news. The same neurotransmitters drive any form of addictive behavior, whether it involves drugs, gambling, food, or sex.

The discovery and release of new and powerful technologies may be laudable as a sign of technological progress; however, in today's political climate, the social media business model has become an instrument of mass destruction and a tool to induce mass psychosis. There is clearly a need for its regulation in order to turn the tide on harmful online practices. While it is extremely important not to endanger freedom of speech, effective regulation may need to include some forms of objective censorship to stop the spread of false information. People who are deliberately disseminating factoids should be penalized. Action needs to be taken to prevent elaborate conspiracy theories from developing that leave vulnerable social media users—such as those experiencing loneliness, isolation, and despair—exposed to false belief systems. In addition, society needs to counteract such propaganda, not just by preventing its existence, but by prioritizing norms and values that foster social harmony rather than conflict; governments should nurture a civic culture that can resist mass psychosis.

CREATING A "GOOD-ENOUGH" SOCIETY

But what is a civic culture, and how easy is it to create one? What steps need to be taken to prevent mass psychosis from developing? How can we ensure that people will act as responsible citizens?

The term "civic culture" is typically used to identify the characteristics of a political culture that make for a well-functioning society.[3] In such societies, there are generally various checks and balances, and people live according to principles including free speech, civil discourse, and the rule of law. However, putting these principles in place is easier said than done. A strong civic culture is a balancing act between contradictory forces, such as the need to respect the rights of the individual and a concern for the public good. Regardless of the outcome of this balancing act between various stakeholders, a civic society is responsive to the interests of its citizens.

In societies with a strong civic culture, fair process is highly valued. There is the expectation that those who govern will treat everyone fairly. This means that in countries with a civic culture, citizens will pay attention to the way public institutions conduct their affairs, manage public resources, and shape public opinion. Additionally, the government must uphold human rights, including civil, cultural, economic, political, or social rights. This includes how people in leadership positions mediate differing interests to reach a broad consensus on what's in the best interests of all.

Moreover, citizens should be able to talk freely about all political topics. They should be actively engaged in local government activities, political parties, and civic institutions, including membership in political associations. This type of culture also requires a tolerance towards opposition parties, with great efforts made to prevent polarization. Good governance will always be top of the agenda, meaning that the decision-makers in the government, private sector, and civil society organizations will be accountable to both institutional stakeholders and the public.

Fundamentally, in a society with a civic culture, citizens don't need to distort or deny their experiences. They don't have a rigid outlook on life and can accurately interpret their experiences and remain open to new ones. Furthermore, they strongly believe in the values of self-determination, freedom, and self-actualization. Liberty will be a key value of such a society, meaning people have a sense of ownership over their lives and are able to retain their sense of self without falling victim to negative, psychotic thinking. By believing in the basic goodness of people, they are able to resist the darkness of mass psychosis.

While commendable, maintaining a positive outlook on life is not an easy task. The threat of mass psychosis induced by demagogue-like leaders always looms. It is far too easy to fall down the rabbit hole of delusionary thinking. As a result, civic cultures will always remain very delicate constructions. This is especially true today, given the potentially destructive power of social media.

THE CRITICAL ROLE OF EDUCATION

In today's society, each citizen is responsible for critically assessing the information provided to them. This involves objectively analyzing and evaluating issues to form a balanced judgment. However, in order to do this, people need to be well-educated. As the Greek philosopher Pythagoras once said, "The beginning of every government starts with the education of our youth." He recognized the fundamental importance of education in creating and sustaining a democratic society. It is clear that the cornerstone to developing and maintaining a civic culture is a country's educational system. Therefore, it is up to a country's policy makers to establish educational systems that emphasize civic culture and include well-designed social studies and civics curricula with a view to fostering responsible citizens. Individuals need to study critical thinking and media literacy, as well as how to separate facts from factoids. History has repeatedly shown that people who receive high-quality civic education from early on are more likely to become engaged and rational citizens throughout their lives.

Education may well provide a source of meaning and purpose in life. Through education, people will be better prepared to engage in reflective thinking and pursue self-discovery.[4] A solid civic education counteracts excessive narcissistic behavior and prevents societal regression. However, the foundation of a civic education requires a willingness to engage in critical self-reflection. People need to take responsibility for their own life with greater clarity, reason, and decency.

This mindset reminds me of an old American Indian story, in which a wise Indian is teaching his grandson about life:

> "A fight is going on inside us," the old Indian said to the boy. "It is a terrible fight. It is a fight between two wolves. One is evil—he is anger, envy, sorrow, regret, greed, arrogance, self-pity, guilt, resentment, inferiority, lies, false pride, superiority, and ego."
>
> The old Indian continued, "The other is good—he is joy, peace, love, hope, serenity, humility, kindness, benevolence, empathy, generosity, truth, compassion, and faith. The same fight is going on inside you—and inside every other person, too."

The grandson thought about it for a minute and then asked his grandfather, "Which wolf will win?"

The old Indian replied, "The one you feed."

With this story in mind, it is my hope that people will "keep their head" despite the tempting pull of mass psychosis and face reality as it is. If they can do so, it will be far less likely that I will encounter more individuals standing on Place Saint Michel in Paris carrying the same "Behold the End Is Near!" sign.

NOTES

1 Carl Jung (1977). *The Symbolic Life: Miscellaneous Writings* (The Collected Works of C. G. Jung, Volume 18). London: Routledge.
2 Heinz Kohut (1971). *The Analysis of the Self.* New York: International Universities Press.
3 Gabriel A. Almond and Sidney Verda (1963). *The Civic Culture: Political Attitudes and Democracy in Five Nations.* Princeton: Princeton Universities Press.
4 Manfred F. R. Kets de Vries (2021). *Quo Vadis: The Existential Challenges of Leaders.* London: Palgrave MacMillan.

2

ARE YOU A SHEEPLE?

Most people are other people. Their thoughts are someone else's opinions, their lives a mimicry, their passions a quotation.

—Oscar Wilde

It is not so much that man is a herd animal, but that he is a horde animal led by a chief.

—Sigmund Freud

A BLENDED CONCEPT

Linguists may recognize that the title of this chapter contains a *portmanteau*—a blend of the sounds and meanings of the words "sheep" and "people." "Sheeple" describes individuals who willingly acquiesce to other people's suggestions without taking a critical stance. They are considered docile, compliant, easily persuaded, and prone to follow the crowd. In other words, sheeple are people who behave in a passive, herd-like manner and have

DOI: 10.4324/9781003427117-3

the potential to engage in the psychotic-like behavior that was the subject of the previous chapter.

The concept of sheeple-like behavior isn't new. In the late 1800s, the French social psychologist Gustav Le Bon referred to the herd behavior of human beings as a way of explaining various crowd phenomena. He wrote, "The crowd is always dominated by considerations of which it is unconscious. . . . The sentiments and ideas of all persons in the gathering take one and the same direction, and their conscious personality vanishes."[1] Le Bon believed that the processes of anonymity, contagion, and suggestibility robbed individuals of their own opinions, values, and beliefs, causing them to behave like sheeple instead of independent thinkers.

Although Le Bon did not extend his theories to the herding behavior seen in the animal kingdom, this is precisely where such behavior is most prominent. In fact, the term "herding behavior" describes the way in which animals act collectively, particularly in the face of danger. In moments of panic, animals, fish, or birds move together as a unit to avoid injury or death, becoming like sheeple. Herd behavior is not enforced by hierarchy or the result of central coordination but arises from the interactions of individual animals within the group. In short, it appears as if an invisible force is driving it.

To better understand this strange herding phenomenon, evolutionary biologist William Hamilton introduced the "selfish herd" theory. He suggested that the emergence of herds is the result of individual animals trying to ensure that predators prey on other members of the group and not themselves.[2] Each animal attempts to reduce the risk of predation on the periphery by moving as close as possible to the center of the fleeing group. Therefore, a herd's form and movement are not the result of coordinated actions, but rather an emergent phenomenon and form of self-preservation, in which each member of the herd is looking out for themselves.

Herd behavior is the result of spontaneous communication processes between members of a species, resulting in a copycat-like process. While sheeple behavior can have positive effects, such as helping animals escape predators, it can also lead to disastrous outcomes, as many animals end up getting injured or trapped.

Although the herd appears to behave like a cohesive, organized unit, it is actually the result of individual members acting in their own self-interest and not to protect the group.

THE ILLUSION OF CONTROL

Human beings are inherently herd animals and social creatures, which has contributed to our success as a species in many ways. Even though we value our individuality, we exist within complex social structures that influence our behavior; we are not the independent decision-makers we like to consider ourselves to be.

While we like to believe that we control our own lives and our choices are based on our own best judgment, certain patterns of behavior extend beyond the individual. We have innate survival instincts in the face of danger; however, we do not always engage in careful and rational thought when responding to these perilous situations and tend to instinctively act in unison.

It is likely that our herd instinct evolved as our prehistoric ancestors evolved into human beings over the course of thousands of centuries. Without it, our predecessors would not have banded together to collect food or fend off dangerous animals. It may explain why humans are inclined to imitate others and sometimes exhibit the same instinctual herd-like behavioral patterns seen more primitively in the animal kingdom.

There are undoubtedly many benefits to living and working cooperatively in groups and sharing knowledge with others. However, much like the panic behavior of animal herds, herd-like behavior in humans can have negative consequences. Overreliance on social information results in people blindly copying one another, and, in certain situations, our evolutionary conditioning may override rational thought. Without even realizing, we may start to behave like sheeple. In particular, when in stressful situations, our instinct is to act immediately, often without taking the time to reflect or gather information that determines the correct course of action. Our fight-or-flight response is activated, and we thoughtlessly follow the crowd. After all, we believe that taking cues from others, like animal herds escaping predators, can save our lives.

THE ROLE OF THE AMYGDALA

When we perceive danger, whether real or imaginary, our brains activate various neurological processes that can trigger herd-like behavior. For instance, the fear of social disapproval and not fitting in can lead to "groupthink," where the desire for group consensus outweighs common sense. Individuals make irrational or non-optimal decisions when they are motivated to conform.

Social psychology and cognitive neuroscience provide firm evidence for sheeple behavior. For example, mirror neurons (the brain cells that fire when we perform an action and when we observe others performing the same action) can explain why individuals blindly follow the crowd. When people see others responding to a situation in a certain way, the mirror neurons in their brain fire, leading them to mimic that behavior without consciously thinking about it.

Similarly, fight-or-flight responses are activated without conscious initiation from the person facing the threat. The amygdala, a region of the brain that processes environmental threats and governs emotional responses, stimulates a physiological response before the frontal lobes have a chance to provide logical reasoning. In other words, our brain favors instinctual reactions over rational, evidence-based observations.

Sheeple behavior can be beneficial when we are in immediate physical danger and need to act quickly to ensure our safety and security.[3] However, this response can be harmful when we surrender our personal values to follow the fears and emotions of the group.

SOCIAL CONTAGION

Even if we are fully aware of the dangers of sheeple behavior, we have all experienced situations where it is easier to follow the crowd than go against it. Sometimes, simply being told that most people hold a certain view can make us change our minds and succumb to group pressure. What is particularly alarming is that we are often unaware that we are behaving like sheeple. By unconsciously internalizing the opinions, feelings, and moods of others, we end up thinking these ideas are our own. This characteristic makes us susceptible to manipulation by those with a specific agenda.

Our desire for social acceptance and fear of rejection makes it extremely difficult to resist group pressure. In fact, there exists research that suggests that a minority of 5 percent can influence the direction of a crowd and mobilize the other 95 percent to follow without even realizing it.[4] This happens when humans pay disproportionate attention to what others say and base their decisions on the opinions of these others.

The dark side of sheeple behavior is that it causes individual judgment and opinion-forming processes to shut down, leading each member to automatically follow the thinking of the group. And this behavioral pattern has a ripple effect, influencing the emotions, dynamics, and thinking of others. This process of social contagion is characterized by a tendency to automatically mimic and synchronize expressions, vocalizations, postures, and movements of others, leading to behavioral convergence. When this occurs, the desire to fit in overrides individual judgment, even though our brains maintain the illusion that our actions are based on our own thinking. At this point we are obliviously flying in autopilot mode.

THE UBIQUITY OF SHEEPLE

Once you begin to take notice, sheeple-like behavior can be observed everywhere. A good example can be found in financial speculation in the stock market, which is driven by greed in the bubbles and fear in the crashes. Interestingly, risky bubbles are caused not by reckless individual risk-taking but by individuals who believe that following the herd is the least risky strategy of all.

Sheeple behavior is also evident in a variety of other settings, including outbursts of mob violence, political movements, religious gatherings, sporting events, riots, strikes, and even consumer preferences such as fashion trends. In each of these instances, individuals adopt opinions based on the actions and viewpoints of others without bothering to consider the evidence for themselves.

SNAKE OIL SALESMEN

Demagogue-like leaders who understand sheeple behavior can easily take advantage of it to gain power. This was particularly evident in Nazi Germany, where the "Führerprinzip" or "leader principle" was taken to the extreme. Adolf Hitler used it to effectively convince people to follow his directions, despite his evil intentions. This is illustrated in the infamous Nazi propaganda film *Triumph of the Will*, directed by Leni Riefenstahl, which portrays Hitler as a savior instilling unity, rather than a man driven by a hatred. The film combines the power of documentary reportage and propaganda in a single, powerful visual force, depicting Hitler as a god-like figure and using tracking shots to show huge, spellbound crowds marching in support of him.

Hitler's actions were clearly intended to elicit a Pavlovian response from the audience. Both the film and his autobiographical manifesto demonstrate that he was a master of propaganda. As he wrote in *Mein Kampf*, "By means of shrewd lies, unremittingly repeated, it is possible to make people believe that heaven is hell—and hell heaven."

Sadly, Hitler's propaganda efforts were extremely effective, and many followed his lead without question. Rudolf Hess, one of his main disciples, reportedly said, "Hitler is Germany and Germany is Hitler. Whatever he does is necessary. Whatever he does is successful. Clearly the Führer has divine blessing." These sentiments were echoed by Joseph Goebbels, Hitler's Minister of Propaganda, who convinced the German people that they were witnessing the greatest miracle in history and a "genius is building the world."[5] These two key figures emphasized that the Führer had complete authority over everything and demanded absolute obedience from all.

Unfortunately, history keeps repeating itself, and leaders continue to take advantage of sheeple behavior. It is now easy to see why people had such unwavering faith in leaders like Joseph Stalin, Benito Mussolini, Mao Zedong, and others, and why they blindly adhered to their bizarre ideologies. Despite the disastrous consequences of these leaders' actions in the past, the pattern of sheeple pattern behavior is still very much alive today. Leaders such as Jair Bolsonaro, Donald Trump, Viktor Orbán, Recep Tayyip Erdoğan, Abdel Fattah El-Sisi, Mohammed bin Salman, Narendra Modi, Ali Khamenei, and Xi Jinping have exploited the very same behavior among populations. And as mentioned before, we watched as Vladimir Putin is manipulating and inundating the Russian population with disturbing propaganda to rationalize his disastrous war in Ukraine. Unfortunately, far too many people believe his strange conspiracy theories and distortions of reality. And anybody, who dares to think differently, ends up in prison or is killed.

The sheeple programming in our brains explains why otherwise sane and sensible people set aside their common sense and underscores that we are not as intelligent and independent as we think we are. It is natural for humans to want to feel part of a community of people with shared cultural and socioeconomic norms. Therefore, it is no surprise that in periods of uncertainty we seek out strong leaders to guide us.

ARE WE BORN SHEEPLE?

Naturally, environmental factors also contribute to sheeple-like behavior. In addition, there are both various neurological factors and developmental processes—such as childrearing and nurturing—that can help explain why people look to leaders to provide protection. Often, leaders are the best authority figures situated to capture the irrational needs, desires, and fears of groups of people.

In his various contributions to developmental psychology, Sigmund Freud highlighted how leaders evoke unconscious associations to primal father figures. (In what was then a more patriarchal age, father figures tended to serve a dominant, authoritative role within a family.) Such figures would hold absolute power and unquestioned authority, making them the natural people to turn to when seeking protection, guidance, and validation. This psychological dynamic makes it easy for leaders to attract followers willing to set aside rational criticism and independent judgment. Instead, these followers, hungry for the leader's approval, are prepared to carry out his or her commands with little regard for any personal or moral judgments.[6] As a result, the leader's word becomes law, and followers begin to believe that all governmental policies, decisions, and offices ought to work towards the leader's objectives.

Worryingly, the influence of social media is contributing to an increase in sheeple behavior. As mentioned in the previous chapter, social networks amplify sensational content that triggers the fight-or-flight response in viewers, and an increasing number of dangerous leaders take advantage of this, preying on people's anxieties in order to achieve their own goals. Fake news has become a popular and persuasive tool. Leaders invent enemies and mobilize sheeple to support all kinds of atrocious behavior. By the time the panic subsides, the reins of power are in the hands of a newly minted despot.

SHEEPLE RESISTANCE

Knowing this sheeple tendency is an integral part of us allows us to be cautious and mindful of its pull. It is easy to slip into herd-like behavior without even noticing. Without vigilance we could easily follow the crowd, losing our individual identity before we know it and becoming psychologically trapped. Only knowledge and resilience will allow us to recognize when demagogue-like leaders are trying to manipulate our inner sheeple, nudging us towards herd-like behavior.

Our ability to reflect is what has driven human progress; however, as social creatures, we must also value our individuality and avoid thoughtlessly acting like sheeple. To eschew such a trap, we need to ask questions, consider our options, and educate ourselves towards making informed decisions, even if it means the risk of looking foolish. It is always easier to follow the herd, but just because everyone else is making a quick decision, it does not mean that they know best. Therefore, when making decisions, we must examine any biases we have and question their origins.

Justifying our choices helps reduce the likelihood of imitating others and accepting ideas without scrutiny. Our greatest challenge is to evaluate our personal beliefs when they conflict with the actions of others. We should welcome different opinions, but at the same time try to understand why they are so different.

Even so, following the crowd often feels like the natural way, and as the phenomenon of groupthink demonstrates, there is always considerable conscious and unconscious pressure to belong to a group. As we are hardwired to want to fit in, it can be difficult to oppose the opinion of the majority. We have to struggle with the belief, irrational as it may be, that large groups of people cannot be wrong.

DEFAULT VERSUS DECISION

It is our challenge to oppose this idea. We should never assume that the larger the group of people involved in a decision, the more likely it is to be correct. History has clearly demonstrated that this can be a serious mistake. We must not allow anyone to tell us what we should think, feel, or do. Instead, we should ask ourselves whether the choices we make are really our own, or whether we have fallen into a sheeple pattern. Once we become aware of our tendency to behave like sheeple, we can make a conscious effort to evaluate our own opinions, and following the crowd will no longer be our default pattern. Daring to do things differently will always be a challenge.

Stress and anxiety can amplify our tendency towards sheeple behavior, especially in situations where we are pressured to act quickly. It's crucial therefore to take the time to reflect and make informed decisions, particularly in stressful environments where it is most easy to be swayed by the crowd. This may mean delaying action until we have assessed the situation and are fully aware of what is happening.

Whenever we feel the pull of sheeple behavior, we should remind ourselves that our capacity for both independent and dependent thought has allowed our species to progress, learn new things, develop, and advance. Of course, this does not mean that we should ignore our heritage, as a society of people all working off completely different scripts with no common themes would be dysfunctional. As social creatures, we are inclined to seek common ground when we gather as a group, and our brains will always rely on a certain degree of groupthink. At the same time, we should remember that the only way to reduce the risk of collective madness or mass psychosis is to stimulate independent thought. It is our lifelong challenge to distinguish between the wisdom and the madness of crowds.

NOTES

[1] https://brocku.ca/MeadProject/Lebon/LeBon_1895/LeBon_1895_02.html

[2] William D. Hamilton (1971). "Geometry for the Selfish Herd," *Journal of Theoretical Biology*, **31**(2), 295–311.

[3] As a caveat, it should be noted that our understanding of these brain patterns is still evolving. Research on the neuroscience of human social behavior has been a relatively neglected topic. Much more research is needed to fully understand these sheeple-like behavior patterns.

[4] University of Leeds. "Sheep in Human Clothing: Scientists Reveal Our Flock Mentality," *ScienceDaily*, 16 February 2008. www.sciencedaily.com/releases/2008/02/080214114517.htm

[5] www.historylearningsite.co.uk/nazi-germany/the-fuehrer-principle/

[6] Sigmund Freud (1921). Group Psychology and the Analysis of the Ego. *The Standard Edition of the Complete Psychological Works of Sigmund Freud*, Volume XVIII. London: International Psycho-Analytical Press; Sigmund Freud (1913–1914). Totem and Taboo and Other Works. *The Standard Edition of the Complete Psychological Works of Sigmund Freud*, Volume XIII. London: International Psycho-Analytical Press.

3

FEELING WRONGED AS A WAY OF LIFE

Let us resolve to be masters, not the victims, of our history, controlling our own destiny without giving way to blind suspicions and emotions.

—John F. Kennedy

I don't believe we can get very far, with leaders who write off half the nation as a bunch of victims who never take responsibility for their own lives.

—Barack Obama

LIVING UNDER A DARK CLOUD

Sheeple behavior can be triggered by various factors. One notable precursor to this phenomenon is the feeling of being wronged. This sense of victimization is well-illustrated in *The Victim*, one of the early novels by Nobel Prize–winning author Saul Bellow.

DOI: 10.4324/9781003427117-4

The book explores one man's victimhood, using the concept of the doppelgänger as a foil. The novel centers around the psychological struggle between two people: the principal character of the novel and his "double." The doppelgänger accuses the protagonist of being responsible for his grim fate, telling him that all his misfortunes, including the loss of his wife and his job, are his own doing.

In the face of these accusations, the protagonist ponders his guilt and responsibility in the matter, prompting his descent into a spiral of paranoia and regret. As time passes, both parties increasingly begin to resemble one another, and victimhood morphs into a dark cloud hovering above them both. It becomes the prism through which they evaluate their life experiences and the main driver of their existence.

THE EVIL GENIUS OF THE DEMAGOGUE

There are many reasons why people feel victimized, the most common being a result of dysfunctional childrearing practices and societal injustices. The two characters in *The Victim* demonstrate how easy it is to enter the haze of victimhood. Many demagogue-like, populist leaders take advantage of and thrive by crafting a world populated by victims and villains.

Again, the mendacious political acrobatics of former US President Donald Trump are a prime example of this behavior. Trump and many leaders of his ilk are experts at preying on people's sense of victimization. They recognize the universality of the victimhood experience and use it to manipulate their audiences to their advantage.

Victimization is rooted in subjective experiences, such as the way people interpret the world around them. Some people perceive themselves as "victims" in circumstances that others would regard as part of the normal vicissitudes of day-to-day life. While victimhood is not necessarily a core part of a person's character, lingering feelings of hurt can easily be activated under the right circumstances, leading to a perpetual sense of feeling wronged.

This sense of victimization applies to both individuals and groups of people. Segments of the population can suffer from collective feelings of victimhood that may stem from objective, lived experiences or social construction. A particular group may believe that harm has intentionally been inflicted on them because of their race, religion, or culture. As a result, a sense of self-perceived collective victimhood develops in their sub-culture.

When members of a population have experienced an extremely traumatic experience, such as war, colonial occupation, or even genocide, it is understandable that they possess a sense of collective victimhood. In the aftermath of such events, feelings of victimhood often linger as people may not have metabolized what has happened. Collective victimhood serves as a foundation for unity and solidarity, and it can even be transmitted between generations.

THE SIRENS OF VICTIMHOOD

It doesn't take much to start feeling like a victim or to find others who share the same feeling. Victimhood spreads rapidly due to the fact that many people have had experiences where they felt unfairly treated. For most, victimhood will only be fleeting; others, however, allow victimhood to transmute into a core element of their personality and develop strong beliefs, attitudes, emotions, and behaviors that are centered around feelings of being victimized.

People who feel victimized often suffer from low self-esteem, a pessimistic outlook on life, a sense of listlessness, and strong feelings of shame, guilt, and self-pity. They blame themselves for their situation and often feel depressed or alienated. Many feel disillusioned with the world, as if life has lost all meaning.

However, a series of negative experiences alone is insufficient to establish victimhood as a core part of an individual's personality. This requires the additional perception that the harm inflicted is undeserved and unjustified, or potentially exacted using immoral or even violent means.

FROM THE INDIVIDUAL TO THE COLLECTIVE

In some cases, both a person's individual rights and the collective rights of a group can be violated. For example, a group of individuals may be economically prevented from taking care of their basic needs, unable to exercise their right to freedom, or restricted from freely expressing their identity. In today's world, there are countless examples of such prejudices and injustices.

Groups retain these experiences in their collective memory. While it is possible that some discriminatory practices are a figment of the imagination, in most instances traumas are based on true events. These transgressions can range from large-scale events, like the loss of a battle or war, ethnic cleansing, or genocide, to long-term, harmful treatment of a particular group, such as slavery or other forms of exploitation.

These communities live with an enduring sense of having been wronged. Such feelings can be contagious and easily affect multiple layers of society. People can directly endure psychological or physical harm, or indirectly experience it through their relationships with other individuals who have been victimized.

Feelings of victimization are often shared and perpetuated to maintain, protect, and repair a group identity. In fact, these feelings may even turn into a kind of "chosen trauma"—a shared mental representation of a major distressing experience that the group suffered—that binds them together.[1] What befell the group is considered a threat to their collective well-being—in some instances, even to the group's survival. Holding on to a chosen trauma turns into the glue that holds them together. Such feelings of solidarity also become a form of self-protection against the fear of future harm.

INDIVIDUAL BEHAVIORAL PATTERNS

One of the possible consequences of a sense of victimhood is the development of a siege mentality. This arises from the belief that an individual or group faces continuous threats. People who feel this way are hyper-vigilant about the world around them, and every experience is scrutinized for negative intentions. They are always on guard, harbor negative expectations towards others, and struggle to trust people they believe are out to get them. Naturally, such an outlook on life results in a cynical perception of people in general.

In addition, people with a victimhood mindset tend to exaggerate little things into big issues, engaging in catastrophizing thought processes. They distort whatever information comes their way, and their cognitive biases lead them to jump to the worst conclusions, despite having very limited information or objective reasoning for them. Under the spell of confirmation bias, they are constantly searching for information that is consistent with their preconceived beliefs, disregarding evidence that does not support their *Weltanschauung*.

Unfortunately, feelings of victimization can trigger patterns of retaliatory behavior, such as cycles of violence directed at those believed to be the cause of their misery. In certain cases, a sense of collective victimhood can escalate into outright violent activities. Subsequently, these individuals may rationalize their actions by claiming they are attempting to prevent future harm or wanting to avenge harm that has already been inflicted. They strongly believe that they need to defend themselves to counteract the immoral and destructive behavior they attribute to their perceived perpetrators. Consequently, they view their violent behavior as justifiable punishment for the harm that has been done to them or strongly believe it to be a means of preventing possible future harm.

Such individuals often have a self-righteous, morally entitled attitude to life. They believe that they have the right to employ any means necessary to ensure their safety. But while doing so, they seem to ignore the moral implications of their actions and exhibit a lack of concern for the traditional safeguards that typically prevent unethical or excessive behavior, such as feelings of shame and guilt. Their sense of collective victimhood functions as the moral bedrock upon which they justify their actions. As they view themselves as victims of perceived injustices, they consider whatever they do to be morally correct. In essence, victimhood becomes a license to engage in immoral and illegitimate acts.

It is evident that these people are masters of rationalization, justifying immoral actions through seemingly logical reasons and explanations. They regard the potential harm they inflict as a form of punishment for what has been done to them and believe they shouldn't be blamed for their actions. This collective perception of victimization serves as a buffer or defense against any negative thoughts and feelings that emerge when they transgress. They are of the opinion that no one has the right to pass moral judgment when they do to others what has been done to them. They may ask themselves how the world ever allowed these terrible things to happen while being simultaneously convinced that traditional moral conventions no longer apply; they believe that they're allowed to do everything within their power to prevent a similar trauma from ever happening again.

In addition, these individuals will resort to the use of more primitive defense mechanisms such as denial, projection, and splitting. For example, they will refute any responsibility for the negative things they have done and always place the blame on others. They will project everything that they don't like about themselves onto others—everyone else is quickly assessed as behaving immorally, unfairly, or selfishly. They will consider others to be the cause of all their unhappiness and deny their own aggressive and destructive impulses, instead projecting them onto other people. They conveniently split the world into "saints" and those who are "pure evil" to help them shore up their self-image. Evidently, this isn't a very nuanced way of looking at the world and only contributes to feelings of helplessness, hopelessness, and despair.

Essentially, these people need their feelings of victimhood to be recognized and validated by others. However, behind this need for affirmation is the desire for the perceived perpetrators of their misery to take responsibility for what they believe has been done to them. They want them to express regret for their wrongdoings.

Another aspect of their personality is their lack of empathy. Whilst preoccupied with their own feelings of being wronged, they are often unable to divert their interest to the suffering of others. They struggle to see things from another person's perspective and feel entitled to behave selfishly. They rationalize this behavior with the belief that they have already had their fair share of suffering and therefore don't need to be attentive to the needs of others.

In addition, people who feel victimized tend to ruminate on their imagined miserable state, repeatedly going over the same information without making an effort to change what is troubling them. Naturally, these constant and repetitive thoughts interfere with their ability to engage in daily tasks, relate to others, and experience positive emotions. Dwelling on negativity, however, doesn't do anything to relieve their distress and improve their mood. These people have become stuck in negative patterns. They replay past hurts, which prevents them from generating new ways of thinking, new behaviors, or new possibilities. Instead, their rumination fuels feelings of anger, firing up a desire for revenge against the imagined perpetrators of their misery.

They also possess what can be called an external locus of control,[2] meaning external forces over which they have no control have determined the trajectory of their life. They easily give up when life doesn't go their way and don't believe that they have the power to change things. In comparison, people who have more of an internal locus of control believe they are responsible for their own success. They believe their own actions, such as hard work and self-determination, dictate what happens in their life.

ORIGINS

The question that arises is: What creates this victim mentality? We can assume that various factors contribute to victimhood becoming a core part of an individual's identity. Most likely, a victim mentality develops because of a person's early negative life experiences. Evidently, the people with whom an individual interacts have a strong influence over who they become. These encounters also determine the kind of mindset a person develops. Attachment patterns, the earliest bonds formed by children with their caregivers, will have a lasting impact that continues throughout life. When caregivers are reliable and available when needed, sensitive to the child's attachment needs, and respond positively to their demands for proximity and support, children feel secure and have positive expectations about the caregivers' availability and responsiveness. In contrast, anxious, insecure attachment can be a significant antecedent for developing a sense of victimhood. In other words, when children are exposed to caregivers who are unavailable or unpredictable, it is more likely that the child (and the future adult) will feel victimized.[3]

Children with autocratic parents are more likely to end up developing this victim mentality. They see themselves as victims because of the way their parents have treated them and have scolded them if they would not follow their rules. Also, it is easy to imagine how a child's sense of self-worth is degraded if they are bullied at school by other children or by their teachers. Consequently, these children develop a self-perception of being a victim throughout their lives, prompting them to look for sympathy and help from others.

Besides these "micro" psychological developmental patterns referring to the individual, "macro" issues also need to be taken into consideration in order to understand a person's sense of victimhood. As is the case for many other human belief systems, a sense of victimization can be the result of major sociocultural influences. For example, members of a specific population group can be subjected to certain discriminatory practices or hear about these practices from close connections. As a result of these influences, a sense of victimhood can become a part of their identity. Here, the role of the media, including the impact of television, radio, and the internet, should not be underestimated.

PASSIVE VERSUS ACTIVE

Whether people who perceive themselves as victims act out or default into inaction depends on the way they internalize victimhood. Whilst some are willing to take action to prevent whatever has happened to them from reoccurring, a more common scenario is inaction. Feeling like a victim sometimes results in individuals taking a passive stand and letting life run its course. These people tell themselves that any efforts to change their situation will fail and conclude that it isn't worth trying.

It is more convenient for such people to remain in a state of passivity. But while they may try to place blame elsewhere or make excuses, they do not take any initiative to change their situation. Of course, their passivity hides angry feelings about a world that always seems to be against them, a world that doesn't seem to care. In addition to their anger, they also feel a sense of resentment towards others who are happy and successful. These feelings will fester if not addressed and result in feelings of depression, isolation, and loneliness. However, such feelings can be turned around if people find a compelling enough reason to do so. That catalyst may be a certain type of leader who may rally them around their sense of victimhood. If so, it doesn't take much to change internal anger into external anger, leading to inappropriate action.

However, none of us should be victims in waiting. Going through life with a victim mentality is not a fulfilling existence. Yielding to it doesn't make life worth living. In that respect, self-pity can be a very dangerous narcotic. It is a losing proposition. It is a form of imprisonment. It is also like wallowing in a dark hole, afraid to explore better alternatives than just feeling like a victim. Instead, the challenge will be to find ways to move from being a victim to becoming a victor.

NOTES

[1] Vamik Volcan (2001). "Transgenerational Transmissions and Chosen Traumas: An Aspect of Large-Group Identity," *Group Analysis*, **31**(1), 79–97.
[2] Julian B. Rotter (1966). "Generalized Expectancies for Internal versus External Control of Reinforcement," *Psychological Monographs: General and Applied*, **80**(1), 1–28.
[3] John Bowlby (1969). *Attachment and Loss*. New York: Basic Books; Mary D. Salter Ainsworth, Mary C. Blehar, Everett Waters, and Sally N. Wall (1978). *Patterns of Attachment: A Psychological Study of the Strange Situation*. Hillsdale, NJ: Erlbaum.

4

THE ACT OF REPARATION

Resentment is like drinking poison and then hoping it will kill your enemies.

—Nelson Mandela

There is not, perhaps, to a mind well instructed, a more painful occurrence, than the death of one we have injured without reparation.

—Samuel Johnson

BEYOND VICTIMHOOD

How can we move beyond victimhood? How can we mediate its influence on people's lives? And what can be done to prevent it? Could victimhood be removed from the social equation in the first place? Sadly, given the world we live in, few people are unaffected by it, whether having been a victim or beneficiary of injustice. As suggested in the previous chapter, victimhood can be looked at as an inherent inclination of the human condition; the art of living

DOI: 10.4324/9781003427117-5

will always contain an element of darkness. The French philosopher Michel de Montaigne succinctly expressed this when he said, "Every man bears the whole stamp of the human condition." Life can be full of bad surprises, and we have all found ourselves in challenging situations.

But paradoxical as it may sound, for some individuals, misery may have its benefits. This can be explored through the concept of "secondary gain"—a term used in psychology to describe the unconscious psychological benefits that may accompany misery. There could be unconscious motivations underlying a complaining mindset. Those individuals might have discovered that portraying themselves as victims can exert a powerful influence on others. They may have come to realize that assuming the role of a victim can elicit sympathy and compassion and result in them being heard, receiving attention, or being understood. It may further motivate those interacting with these individuals to offer assistance and support. In some circumstances victim mode can also make "the victim" feel morally superior, special, or even serve as a shield against criticism for their potentially questionable actions.

While this kind of victim mindset may offer comfort, adopting this approach to life can be a form of self-sabotage, hindering its victims from living a fulfilled life. After all, if a significant amount of time and energy is spent on complaining, how can life truly be fulfilling? Frequently, people with this mindset tend to adopt a passive attitude to life, allowing it to simply pass them by.

It would be far more constructive for those who wallow in victimhood to ask themselves whether they could do anything to improve their situation. Rather than accepting victimhood as their destiny or an inescapable reality, they should take constructive steps to transform their lives.

If certain socialization processes can instill a victimhood mindset in individuals, should it not follow suit that other forms of socialization have the potential to reverse this damage? Must these people be solely defined by negative experiences? Wouldn't it be more productive to build upon these traumatic experiences and use them as a foundation for personal growth and improvement?

It is within our power to use negative experiences to create a more positive and hopeful attitude to life; victims could be empowered to take control of their lives as opposed to passively accepting their circumstances.

VICTIM TO "VICTOR"

People with a victim mentality must understand that blaming others for their misery offers only temporary relief from their pain. In the long run, it only fosters feelings of helplessness and hopelessness. A victim mentality obscures their ability to see the blessings that each day brings, and as a result, their spirit becomes poisoned rather than nourished. As long as they perceive themselves as victims, they will remain trapped in that role.

The key to transcending the victimization mindset is to change the perception of self from victim to that of survivor, in essence to see oneself as a "victor." Although these individuals' characters may have been influenced by unfortunate events in their past, they should not merely accept the status quo. For the sake of their mental well-being, it is more beneficial to take charge, assume responsibility, and claim ownership of their lives.

What these people need to bear in mind is that a victim mindset can hinder future development opportunities. By refusing to accept personal responsibility for their circumstances, they greatly limit their power to further progress and grow. In fact, persisting in the victim role can become a self-fulfilling prophecy, as individuals inadvertently become the architects of their own victimhood.

The first step in the healing process is recognizing the extent to which their behavior is self-sabotaging. The constant anticipation that bad things can happen at any moment may lead them to turn the passive into the active, effectively making their fears materialize. This behavior could be seen as a convoluted attempt to delude themselves that they have a modicum of control over their situation. Nevertheless, it is a highly self-destructive form of control.

Instead, these people need to ask themselves what role they are playing in contributing to their own misery. What degree of responsibility do they have in the matter, and what is within their own control? If they're willing to address this question, they may discover that they actually possess significant power to choose how they respond and therefore a certain responsibility for their situation. By taking action to address their problems, they will cease to be victims of circumstance and, instead, transform into agents of change—they can position themselves as survivors.

The challenge for people who feel victimized is to let go of their grudges or, in fact, anything they believe contributes to their misery. It is up to them to embrace a more hopeful, less helpless outlook. They must acknowledge that choosing martyrdom isn't a positive or productive means of navigating life. Moreover, they may have become so blinded by their perceived victimhood that they subject those who interact with them to a victim's role as well.

The starting point for change lies in recognition of the reasons behind their emotions and feelings. They must question why they think the world is against them and make a conscious effort to divert the thoughts that inevitably lead to a sense of victimhood. In order to unearth the underlying causes of their preoccupation with victimhood, they must first obtain a deeper understanding of their thought processes. Without self-knowledge, there will always be a tendency to operate on autopilot and act without thought.

Unfortunately, it may be the easier and more likely choice to dwell on feelings of victimhood. They struggle to think independently or objectively. Therefore, an important step in the change process is recognizing all that is debilitating of a victim mentality: Is life happening to them, or do they have the capacity to actively shape their own lives?

By being attentive to how their thoughts and feelings shape the stories they tell themselves, they can proactively adjust their behavior. With more awareness as to the reasons behind their thought patterns, individuals can more consciously decide how to respond in order to achieve more favorable outcomes. Their task is to draw their unconscious thoughts into consciousness, enabling them to shift their focus from feeling victimized to concentrating on what they can control.

UNCOVERING THE ROOTS

Exploring the origins of their self-limiting beliefs may be the crux of overcoming a victim mindset. This involves an inner journey to gain a greater insight into what lies beneath the sense of powerlessness that colors their outlook on life. They need to be prepared to uncover the roots of their victim mentality, understanding how past life experiences and memories have contributed to their distorted perceptions, thoughts, and beliefs. This deeply personal, introspective process may require them to unpack repressed childhood experiences. Only by confronting these memories can they gain insight into the origins of certain behavioral traits and understand why victimhood has become a core part of their identity.

Embarking on this inner journey will be crucial to their healing and transformation process. Only through self-knowledge can individuals put an end to self-pitying behavior. In fact, by acquiring this insight, they may discover that a "victor" is essentially a "victim" who has decided to take action and address the issues that they believe are victimizing them, instead of simply complaining about them. Eventually, they may come to realize that they will remain a victim for as long as they willingly inhabit that role.

They may come to recognize that a victimhood mindset originates from learned perceptions that are built upon old memories of pain and pleasure, or how significant life experiences have been interpreted and emotionally processed—or not processed—over time. Little by little, this process of self-exploration will reveal the extent to which the way they have been interpreting and defining their experiences has shaped their outlook on life. They may also discover that their adaptive coping mechanisms are now dysfunctional and no longer helpful, and that it may be time to discard them.

As they attempt to reshape and reframe their thoughts, they must learn to think independently, rather than as passive victims of their circumstances. In fact, holding on to victimhood renders them susceptible to exploitation, notably by populist, demagogue-like leaders who are adept at manipulation tactics. They need only rattle their sense of injustice to bring out the worst, most submissive parts of themselves. This is highly relevant in the battle to resisting sheeple-like responses and the dangerous lure of demagogue leaderships.

The hope is that on the journey towards self-knowledge, these people will realize that whining and blaming others for whatever they believe is wrong in their lives will not make their troubles disappear. After all, it is difficult to have agency over their lives while harboring the belief that others are responsible for what happens to them. If they embark on this inner journey with an open and receptive mind, they will no longer indulge in wallowing in victimhood. With increased insight, they will learn to release the perceived injustices of racism, politics, bullies, "imperfect" parents, ex-wives, ex-husbands, unreliable friends, elitist people, financial manipulators, immigrants, or anything else for their problems. They will no longer be tempted to make statements like, "I'm this way because of my father," "I'm like this because I was bullied by my teacher," "I act the way I do because people like me are hated by others," or "I'm this way because foreign influences took advantage of me." They will no longer be seduced by slogans used by demagogue-like leaders, claiming that they will "drain the swamp." Having acquired some self-knowledge, they will be able to recognize manipulation when they see it.

REFRAMING THE FUTURE

Other aspects of victim mentality can be unlearnt. Once individuals understand that victimhood thrives on negative thoughts, they can take the first active step to derail such thinking. This act of reframing can be regarded as a milestone in creating their own new reality. It will lead them to realize that healthier coping mechanisms can be applied, and they can regain control over the direction of their life. Step by step, these individuals can learn how to design life on their own terms, creating their own reality by focusing on what they *can* control and letting go of what they can't.

Therefore, if these people start focusing on what's good in their life, this change in mindset can also evolve into a more positive kind of self-fulfilling prophecy. Instead of looking for the bad in every situation, they will make an attempt to find the silver lining in every challenge. The moment they stop blaming the world for their misery is the moment they shift from being a victim to a victor. This is their route to self-empowerment. With a transformed outlook on life, they are able to see that a sense of self-determination is available for everyone. With this newfound outlook, life may start working in their favor, and victimhood will no longer be seen as the only option.

As this journey involves a great deal of self-reflection, these individuals may find it difficult to navigate this process of change alone. If they want to explore the root causes of their victim mentality, seeking the support of trusted loved ones, psychotherapists, or coaches could be beneficial. These people can help them to identify what is holding them back and guide them in exploring the reasons behind their feelings of helplessness and hopelessness. Additionally, they can provide support in developing a more self-compassionate outlook.

FORGIVENESS

An important part of the process of unlearning victimhood is being able to forgive what has happened. Forgiveness is an important step in letting go and moving forward. It is not only about releasing feelings of bitterness but also about relinquishing the anger they may be holding towards others. However, forgiveness should not be mistaken for justifying the actions of others. It is an internal, mental act of letting go of painful feelings.

Genuine forgiveness sets people free from the prison of victimhood that colors their day-to-day experiences. In fact, forgiveness becomes a gift that they give to themselves, empowering them to find inner peace by moving beyond the pain they have experienced. However, forgiveness does not absolve the perpetrators of their actions, nor does it mean forgetting what happened.

Any attempt at forgiveness will be a truly courageous act for many. It should not be considered conceding defeat but a step towards freedom. In contrast, continuing to play the victim role and choosing to cling to bitterness, anger, and the belief of being wronged (often without investigating the other person's intentions) is time- and energy-consuming and obstructs progress in life.

Sadly, many people hold onto bitterness or resentment under the false belief that it will force others to change. They want others to accept blame, take responsibility, or apologize for their hurt. However, it would be much more beneficial for them to recognize that they, too, may have hurt someone and that such experiences are a part of life. In fact, everyone, at some point in their life, will either need or have to offer forgiveness.

EMPATHY AND COMPASSION

Instead of poisoning their mind with resentful thoughts, people who feel victimized could also benefit from practicing empathy and compassion. They should recognize that they're not the only ones suffering and that others also experience negative emotions. Holding onto fear, guilt, hate, rage, and self-pity will keep them captive and reinforce their identification with victimhood. Instead of resenting others and thus remaining bound to them, they need to realize that empathy and compassion towards others can be a healing force. By being empathic, they will gain greater awareness of other people's emotions and try to understand how they feel. In addition, practicing compassion enables them to respond with a genuine desire to help others.

Showing empathy, compassion, and forgiveness towards those whom these people view as wrongdoers can be liberating, whereas maintaining their state of victimhood may well become increasingly futile, harmful, and a waste of time. Not only does it repel other people, but it also robs them of the possibility of realizing true happiness. By letting go of these negative feelings, they can escape their state of captivity and avoid reinforcing their identity as victims.

KINDNESS

Another remedy for the victim mentality is engaging in acts of kindness. All too often, people with a victim mentality tend to believe everything in the world revolves around them and their pain. To transcend this self-centered perspective, they would benefit from performing altruistic deeds for others, which can also help them overcome feelings of helplessness and hopelessness. Making a conscious choice to be kind to others is a source of empowerment, fostering a sense of control over their own lives. If these self-perceived victims replace their perceived suffering with acts of kindness and are prepared to help other people, they are likely to significantly improve their well-being. As counterintuitive as it may seem, the more they feel deprived, the more essential it is to give. Offering kindness is the most effective way to dispel feelings of self-pity.

GRATITUDE

What appears to be a major contributing factor to this victim mentality is the feeling of lacking something—the sense that there is never enough of something. Gratitude comes into play when one shifts their focus from a sense of emotional deprivation to embracing abundance. All too often, the belief that something is missing—be that explanation, apologies, affection, justice, or any other negative emotion—has trapped these individuals in a cycle of negative thoughts and self-pity. If they were prepared to actively practice gratitude and concentrate on the blessings in their life, they could cultivate a more positive mindset. It is essential for them to realize that a life lived with kindness and gratitude far surpasses one centered on resentment and bitterness. In other words, the quickest way to stop feeling like a victim is to adopt an attitude of gratitude and focus on the good that's happening.

To change their outlook on life, individuals drawn to victimhood should make a habit of asking themselves, "What am I grateful for today?" or "What good things have happened in my life today?" Gratitude, in essence, is the conscious acknowledgment of what brings joy in the present moment. When people stop obsessing about their own concerns and consider the bigger picture, they begin to recognize how lucky they really are.

FOCUS ON THE COLLECTIVE

The experience of being wronged is not always solely attributed to personal trauma. Feelings of victimization can also stem from distressing collective experiences. For instance, people of different ethnic or religious backgrounds may have encountered discrimination. In such cases, psychological healing cannot be fully achieved or addressed at an individual level. When individual traumas form part of larger societal traumas, the process of letting go and moving on takes on a distinct character. In these situations, healing becomes more of a collective endeavor. Therefore, in addition to addressing healing on a personal level, there is a need for a more public, societal process of reconciliation. Attention must be given to the events and experiences that have affected the collective.

Failing to achieve reconciliation creates an environment of discord where demagogue-like, populist leaders are able to take advantage of negative mindsets, particularly considering how easily the sense of victimhood spreads both temporally and geographically. Such leaders are particularly skilled at manipulating feelings of victimhood on the public stage. To prevent this from happening, it is essential for people to move beyond denial.

MOVING BEYOND DENIAL

While holding onto feelings of victimhood inhibits progress, denying the harm that has been inflicted on a societal level is equally futile. Ignoring injustices committed leaves victims in a lifeless existence, burdened by buried trauma and painful memories. As Holocaust survivor and Nobel Prize winner Elie Wiesel once said, "Silence encourages the tormentor, never the tormented." In the face of injustice, action is required. The victims of injustice need not only the will to fight back but also the necessary skills and resources to do so.

Of injustice, the philosopher George Santayana wisely said, "Those who cannot remember the past are condemned to repeat it." Hence, when bad things have happened to certain groups of people, simply whitewashing the damage is not enough. People need to transcend denial and confront their traumatic experiences. Failure to do so will likely result in a repetition of those atrocities; history has taught us this repeatedly.

However, facing up to these atrocities and the associated memories and emotions can be very stressful and challenging. It is crucial to be on guard to withstand the unconscious pull of suppression and forgetfulness. Regardless of the nature of the traumatic experience, its history must be preserved. The experience should be integrated into the realm of self-reflective memory. In other words, people should come to terms with the past and understand the importance of encouraging a culture of shared remembrance. However, it is necessary to acknowledge the characteristics of the cultural and social atmosphere that allowed these atrocities to take place. Understanding the context in which these events occurred is essential, even if it does not excuse or justify what happened.

MOURNING

Mourning will be an integral part of the process of remembrance that allows people to arrive at new beginnings and metabolize what has happened. It offers a mechanism through which people can confront the wounds of the past and pave the way for a new and inclusive future. Engaging in public discourse as part of this process can also have a therapeutic effect. In addition, to prevent the recurrence of past injustices, some form of conflict transition, such as redress and reparation, is necessary.

In some cases, victims of atrocities may not be looking for real closure but to perpetuate what has happened to them. For these individuals, victimhood might have become a means to gain economic and political concessions. They may argue that settlements are rightfully owed to them, given the experiences they have endured.

Apart from these exceptional cases, it is crucial to listen to the collective voices of victims in order to facilitate a transition from conflict. To enable this process, these people need to bear witness; otherwise, they will continue to relive their traumatic experiences and remain unable to move beyond the injustice they have experienced. If their voices have not been heard, they may well remain feeling violated, cheated, confused, scared, insecure, ashamed, guilty, and helpless. To achieve greater peace of mind and any form of resolution, they need to address the traumatic experiences. Remembrance can therefore serve as a means to prevent the recurrence of despicable acts. Dedication to breaking cycles of violence will be the only means of fostering peace.

Furthermore, injustice can also fracture the bonds that tie individuals to society at large. Trauma isolates groups of people but also brings shame and stigma. Therefore, in order for society to effectively function in the future, it is essential to recreate and nourish a sense of community. Restoring the survivors' faith in humanity requires rebuilding their connections with the larger community. But to achieve this outcome, it is essential to embark on a process of reconciliation.

RECONCILIATION

Reconciliation refers to the restoration of fractured relationships by overcoming feelings of grief, pain, and anger. It is a process driven by society that involves mutual acknowledgment of past suffering, with the goal of changing destructive attitudes and behaviors into more constructive ones. It provides a platform for healing the relationships between groups of people who have been wronged, addressing their spiritual, psychological, social, intrapersonal, and interpersonal realms. Additionally, it can be seen as a process that empowers victims to adopt a more hopeful outlook for the future. Thus, it can be a highly effective way to change their perception regarding those who have been blamed for their misfortune.

Essentially, reconciliation is a psychological transformation process of the collective self. It means that the party responsible for the traumatic experiences and the party that has been traumatized are prepared to address issues of justice and truth. Both parties need to be willing to face the true ugliness of what has happened. It is important to add, however, that effective reconciliation needs to be a staged process, although its specific stages may vary.

Reconciliation usually starts with an effort to replace the fear of the other party with a form of non-violent coexistence. This phase requires building confidence and trust, fueled by compassion and empathy. An important part of this process is that both parties express the range of emotions caused by the offense. Both parties also need to try to understand why the event occurred and what the contributing factors were. Without finding some rationale, it is very hard to put things to rest.

Furthermore, the victimized party needs to feel a sense of security, knowing that the hurtful behavior will not occur again. This assurance could come in the form of a sincere apology and reconciliation or by implementing specific measures to prevent any recurrence in the future. Finally, as part of this staged process, the victimized party must also make the conscious choice to let go of the past.

Letting go is a decision; it involves making a promise to stop ruminating and dwelling on what has happened. This step includes refraining from continually bringing up the incident and using it against the other party. Naturally, this step isn't easy, and if the two parties haven't properly invested in the preceding stages of reconciliation, they might find themselves simply unable to let go.

Reconciliation tends to be a lengthy process that requires both parties to build trust, establish a non-violent relationship, and learn to live cooperatively. The challenge lies in breaking the prevailing cycle of violence and establishing peace, justice, fairness, healing, and forgiveness. It involves overcoming personal enmities, recovering cultural identities, and fostering productive relationships within and between communities.

PRIVATE OR PUBLIC?

It is important to remember that reconciliation doesn't necessarily mean forgiveness, however closely the two are connected. They are not the same: Forgiveness is a conscious, deliberate decision to release feelings of anger, resentment, or vengeance towards someone, regardless of whether the offender has apologized or asked for forgiveness. It means letting go of the desire to punish the other person or demand restitution from them. Thus, forgiving is a process of inner healing for an individual—a deeply private and internal process where they work through their emotional wounds. It involves gaining an understanding of what has happened, rebuilding a sense of safety, and releasing any grudges they may be holding. However, forgiveness doesn't necessarily require a response from the person who caused the harm. The offender may not even be aware that they have been forgiven.

Reconciliation, on the other hand, is a collective process and a public endeavor. It entails restoring broken or damaged relationships between groups of people. For example, it could encompass the political healing within a nation, where two groups that were formerly in conflict with each other attempt to repair the wounds of the past. The South African Truth and Reconciliation Commission, which addressed the atrocities of the apartheid regime, and the Truth and Reconciliation Commission of Canada, which dealt with injustices against Indigenous peoples, are prominent examples of such efforts. Reconciliation is about the restoration of fractured relationships by overcoming feelings of grief, pain, and anger. In this sense, reconciliation lies at the heart of building and maintaining peace in a society, especially between divided communities.

Unlike forgiveness, reconciliation requires the cooperation of both parties. In this interpersonal process, both parties engage in dialogue about what has transpired, exchange stories, and express their hurt. The offenders need to apologize. If so, the victimized party listens for true signs of remorse, which is a critical element if the releasing of grudges is to occur. This makes reconciliation a far more complicated process. It revolves around building trust and positive relationships, with the assurance that there will be no harm in the future. It can be seen as the foundation upon which individual forgiveness can be built.

TESTIMONIALS

If the survivors of an atrocity are able to testify about what has happened to them, there is a possibility that a sense of connection with the other party can be restored. However, this psychological restoration and healing can only occur if a space is provided for the survivors to feel heard. Thus, an environment needs to be created where every detail of the traumatic event can be re-experienced in a safe and supportive setting.

Although survivors may feel they have lost their faith in humanity, and that common human decency has been irretrievably destroyed, it is through the process of giving testimony that a relationship can be rebuilt. This requires the party responsible for the atrocities to acknowledge what they have done. By giving testimony, the victims will be able to reclaim lost parts of themselves and embrace common humanity.

To initiate the process of reconciliation, an extensive examination of the extent and nature of the harm done must be conducted. It also necessitates an investigation into accountability and the enabling factors of the atrocity. Through this process, both sides are able to acknowledge what happened in the past and try to understand each other's narratives. This establishes a common frame of reference that enables and encourages both parties to acknowledge the past, confess any wrongs that have been inflicted, reexamine the experiences under controlled conditions, mourn the losses, validate the pain and grief, receive empathy and support, and hopefully restore the broken relationship.

Reconciliation with the past is an essential part of moving forward on the healing journey. One of the benefits of this process is that it aims to create equity and equality by reducing the victims' sense of injustice. It involves building bridges between opposing parties and repairing fractured relationships to make it possible to live harmoniously in the future. In other words, reconciliation helps break the past cycle of violence from the past, build a more peaceful shared future, and sustain peace over time. However, forming peaceful relations based on mutual trust, acceptance, cooperation, and consideration of needs takes time. The mourning process alone can be a very lengthy endeavor.[1]

However, a successful process of reconciliation should ultimately lead to a collective healing process that includes forgiveness. Significant apologies and compensation may be needed. It is also possible that certain conflicts are asymmetrical in terms of how the parties involved carried out their harmful acts. In such instances, it is essential that the "bigger" perpetrator is willing to take greater responsibility for the harm that has been done. This is just one of the legacies of demagogue-like leaders in the aftermath of their reign.

COMING FULL CIRCLE

Life is not really rosy, and setbacks are an integral part of social existence. Individuals and groups tend to go through cycles that include not only phases of conflict and animosity but also phases of cooperation and relative harmony. This repetitive pattern between conflict and cooperation arises from the fact that humans are social animals who must cooperate with other group members to confront external dangers while simultaneously competing to survive. Competition for scarce resources, for example, can lead to inevitable conflict and situations that result in victimization.

The question at hand is how to minimize the human inclination towards conflict, whether on an individual or societal level. Conflict breeds feelings of victimization and a subsequent desire for revenge that can be harmful to the well-being of others. If conflicts escalate further, retaliatory harm may only contribute to a pervasive sense of mass victimization.

A perpetual victimhood mindset only perpetuates a view of the world through dark-tinted glasses. However, if both parties were to adopt a different perspective, they might discover that the "others" are not necessary evil and that not everyone within their own group is faultless. They may come to the realization that they're all human and imperfect.

People who experience a sense of victimhood need to realize that as long as they attribute the cause of their problems to external factors and place blame on others for their suffering, they will remain stuck in their state of victimhood. If, however, they're prepared to take action and work to change their self-perception as a victim of circumstances, they will not only transition to the role of survivor but also become a role model. They will serve as an inspiration to those still stuck in the victim mindset. The choice is theirs—they must ask themselves whether they desire a life of self-fulfillment or to live in a world colored by self-pity.

To overcome a sense of victimhood, individuals need to embark on two different journeys. The first one is directed inward towards self-exploration, helping them to reconcile their personal suffering. The second journey, which pertains to mass injustices, is directed outward, involving reconciliation and a sense of forgiveness towards others.

Undertaking these journeys will offer significant benefits, as those who come out on the other side are far less likely to be manipulated by individuals with malicious intent. In our present-day society, this is no small matter. There are too many leaders around the world who are ready and willing to exploit the feelings of victimization in people and manipulate them for their own political agendas. Hence, a word of caution: *caveat emptor*!

NOTE

[1] Alexander Mitscherlich (1975). *The Inability to Mourn: Principles of Collective Behavior.* New York: Grove Press.

5

THE POPULIST LEADERSHIP THREAT

It has been very truly said that the mob has many heads, but no brains.

—Antoine Rivarol

The secret of the demagogue is to make himself as stupid as his audience so they believe they are clever as he.

—Karl Kraus

THE RISE OF POPULISM

In the preceding chapters, I have expressed my concern regarding people's tendency to adopt herd-like behavior patterns. I have pointed out that situations of high uncertainty create ideal conditions for a population to regress and be exploited by leaders with demagogue-like characteristics. This, I have suggested, will be all

DOI: 10.4324/9781003427117-6

the more the case when people feel victimized. It is at this juncture that populism enters the frame.

The political landscape of the last decades clearly illustrates a surge in the popularity of populist politics, authoritarian policies, and autocratic personalities. On a global scale, liberal democracy isn't faring too well, as many countries' democracies have become increasingly plagued by dysfunction and polarization. Several countries that were once considered liberal democracies now show signs of illiberalism and de-institutionalization. We have also seen a decline in the quality of democracy in less established democratic countries, with many appearing to be democracies in name alone. This has resulted in the rise of authoritarianism, with powerful autocrats like President Xi Jinping of China and President Vladimir Putin of Russia serving as prominent role models.

Some people have even argued that democracy is now a form of government that is passé, only leading to chaos and stagnation. These turns of events have eroded confidence in the ability of liberal governments to make sound decisions. It is not surprising that some are advocating for a concentration of power in governance as a path to progress.

Populism has played a significant role in these disturbing developments, emerging as one of the "buzzwords" of our times. Its rise in popularity is a threat that needs to be taken very seriously and a concern that has motivated the dialogue these essays initiate. Populist movements are challenging the fundamental values of liberal democracy, a form of government founded on Enlightenment principles, which celebrates reason, individual liberty, a belief in scientific progress, secularism, tolerance, and freedom of thought. In contrast, populist principles embrace a more absolutist and intolerant notion of majoritarian popular sovereignty.

Populism poses a direct challenge to liberal democracy, primarily by exhibiting contempt for pluralistic ideas, such as the recognition of differing opinions. Additionally, many of the proponents of populism are suspicious of established institutions and openly express their desire to "drain the swamp" by eliminating them. However, there can be an element of truth in their accusations, as liberal capitalist institutions are not free from faults. Great financial inequities are often a significant contributing factor to people's discontent.

Despite its imperfections, when liberal democracy disappears, there is a high probability that consensus and compromise will be replaced by unyielding polarization, animosity, and hatred. Still, despite the dangers that populism brings, many are seduced by the alluring promises of populist leaders who pretend to champion their interests. Regrettably, too many people are prepared to sacrifice the very idea of liberal democracy at this altar of populism.

Why is this happening? What makes populism so attractive? What lies behind the captivating allure of these populist leaders, and what can be done to halt their rise? It is evident that to address the dangers of populism, we need to gain a better understanding of the cultural and socio-psychological processes that underpin its emergence and sustain its continued existence.

THE POPULIST MUDDLE

An effective way to begin answering these questions is to understand what populism truly entails. Populism is a somewhat contested concept that can be interpreted in many different ways. In essence, it can be viewed as an ideology, a movement, a syndrome, a discourse style, or a political strategy associated with people experiencing a decline in social status or economic strain. It can even encompass feelings of nationalist nostalgia.

In its original form, populism is an ideology that posits politics should be a reflection of the general will of the people. It considers society as fundamentally divided into two homogenous and antagonistic groups: the "pure people" versus the "corrupt elite." The "pure people" view their ideology as morally absolute, imagining themselves pitted against a privileged, elite class of oppressors.

However, a closer examination of populism reveals it to be an archaic, collectivist, even tribal ideology, where proponents exist in a stark and simplistic world of "good" versus "evil." This perspective allows little room for nuanced thinking and compromise.

They aren't interested in finding middle ground, yet they offer few or no constructive solutions for the future. Their only plans seem to revolve around dismantling existing structures, akin to breaking toys so that nobody else can play with them.

Typically, populist ideas are implemented by charismatic leaders who appeal to the masses using anti-elite and people-centric messages. In their effort to sideline established institutions, these individuals argue that they are the real representatives of the people. According to their narrative, everybody associated with these institutions is illegitimate and not to be trusted. To drive their arguments, they skillfully employ extreme language, well aware that it arouses strong emotional responses and gets people's adrenaline flowing.

Populist movements reiterate how people are disenfranchised and victimized because the establishment is failing to treat ordinary citizens fairly. By using their Manichean ideological framework, they paint a world in which the "pure people" and the "corrupt elite" are caught in a life-and-death struggle. Support for these populist forces hinges on effectively politicizing negative partisanship in relation to mainstream political parties. After all, everybody enjoys a story where the underdog rises up to challenge the establishment.

Populist leaders attempt to construct new electoral platforms that exploit these antagonistic ideas to raise awareness of issues that affect selected segments of the voting public. In an effort to rectify these perceived injustices and grievances, populist leaders advocate for a hierarchical, autocratic system, which they claim is the answer to everyone's prayers. However, this Manichean ideology disregards the legitimacy and even the possibility of individual freedom and personal choice.

Despite their distinct worldview, populist leaders also claim to be democratic. They base much of their rhetoric on the notion that the existing political system has ignored, neglected, or outright opposed the interests of the common people. Their concept of democracy is rooted in majoritarian and illiberal terms. This paradox highlights another crucial quality of these proponents of populism: their disdain for the fundamental norms and institutions of a liberal democracy. As a result, they're quick to discard constraining principles such as the rule of law, minority rights, checks and balances, free speech, freedom of the press, the moral legitimacy of any opposition, acceptance of the separation of powers, judicial independence, and term limits for elected officials. Their absolutist approach to governance implies a refusal to share power, and any victory by their opponents is perceived not just as a political misfortune but as an existential threat demanding extreme measures. When an opponent is successful, this seems to justify discarding any sense of forbearance and restraint, as illustrated by Trump's earlier mentioned refusal to accept the outcome of the 2020 presidential election.

RIGHT- AND LEFT-WING POPULISM

Interestingly, contemporary populism encompasses both the right-wing and left-wing extremist movements on the political spectrum. Both employ similar psychological strategies; the only difference is the content of their narratives. Right-wing populists typically emphasize nationalistic ideologies, stressing the importance of order, structure, predictability, and conservatism. On the other hand, left-wing populists are more concerned with economic, ethnic, and racial inequality, drawing on narratives that are disguised as well-intentioned, utopian social justice theories that advocate for state power, wealth redistribution, and collectivism.

It becomes apparent that nationalism, racism, ethnocentrism, and xenophobia are typical right-wing ideologies, whereas identity politics, woke-ism, cancel culture, language control, and political correctness are equally dangerous strategies that typify left-wing utopian agendas. In essence, right-wing populism tends to focus on the denigration of the "other," while left-wing populism leans towards emphasizing the divide between the "haves" and the "have-nots."

In economic terms, populism perceives economic matters as a zero-sum game, a battle between clear winners and losers. Right-wing populists are primarily concerned about economic tensions between nations or ethnic groups. Conversely, left-wing populists consider economic matters to be more of a class struggle.

Nevertheless, both groups regard socioeconomic problems as the malevolent designs of foreigners, minorities, and insidious elites, rather than challenges that are inevitable in an indifferent universe.

Despite their differences, both right-wing and left-wing populists share a rather autocratic orientation towards governance. In fact, the totalitarian excesses of right-wing populism are no less disconcerting than those of left-wing populism. Additionally, both ideological orientations capitalize on the human tendency to regress and seek savior-figures in times of stress. In such situations, people's dependency and sheeple-like behavior play a central role. Indeed, both historical and contemporary populist movements, such as Marxism, fascism, cancel culture, Antifa, and woke-ism, are explicitly designed to exploit these fundamental inclinations in human nature.

People's fascination with populism stems from their frustration with feeling helpless and powerless. They are confused and convinced that the current political actors are failing to address their needs, leading them to reject mainstream political parties. However, this also sets them up to be easily swayed by confidence tricksters and charismatic charlatans. As the political journalist Alexander Cockburn once ironically suggested:

> No chord in populism reverberates more strongly than the notion that the robust common sense of an unstained outsider is the best medicine for an ailing polity. Caligula doubtless got big cheers from the plebs when he installed his horse as proconsul.[1]

CONTRIBUTING FACTORS

The current surge in populism appears to be a result of the interplay of various factors, some of which mutually reinforce one another. As progressively explored in earlier chapters, times of crisis and intense feelings of anxiety about the world provide an ideal breeding ground for populist leaderships. These actors are masters at oversimplifying complex issues, manipulating people's feelings, and capitalizing on their gullibility.

As we live in an age of uncertainty and change, in which many people are deeply concerned about the state of the world and what is to come, many of these concerns are instrumental to populist agendas. This is where the victimhood mentality that was the subject of the previous chapter comes into play, as people's sense of perceived injustice and inequality is both cultivated and manipulated in the national psyche.

FOLLOW THE MONEY

Economic factors play an important role in the rise of populism. The financial crises of the past decades have been instrumental in fueling these populist political movements. These economic downturns not only exacerbated income inequality but also underscored the degree to which globalization and technology have impacted people's lives. Consequently, there is an element of truth in the claims of populist leaders regarding the perceived betrayal of "the people" by the "elites." Income and wealth inequality has contributed to an increasing social divide between the top earners and the rest of the population, intensifying sociocultural grievances.

Prominent among these sociocultural grievances are concerns about increasing immigration, the decline of traditional values, the mobilization of women, and the role of so-called minority groups. Certain segments of the population strongly believe that these groups have become the beneficiaries of significant economic advantages, fueling a widespread sense of distrust towards those who appear different. These sentiments have collectively contributed to feelings of discontent and divisions among citizens, both within and between many nations.

The Threat of Change

In this environment of heightened anxiety, we cannot overlook the profound impact of technological change. Large segments of the population are increasingly fearful that their lives and even their minds will be radically affected by emerging technologies. Many are anxious about the rise of autonomous robots and artificial intelligence and fear that they will not be able to adapt. The pace at which these changes are occurring only adds to their apprehension. They fear that these new technologies will render their jobs obsolete, leading to feelings of redundancy and insecurity.

Technology and globalization are intrinsically linked, as the introduction of new technologies in various regions alters the competitive landscape of many countries. Globalization has facilitated easier access to knowledge for countries, but it has also contributed to major structural changes where some countries have benefited and others have faced losses. Naturally, these changes have affected the job market, leaving certain sectors of the workforce feeling vulnerable and unprotected. As a result, it is understandable why a large number of people in established liberal democracies have become increasingly anxious, divided, and distrustful of global developments. These changes have heightened insecurity among the less educated, often rural population in comparison to the more privileged, educated urban population. Consequently, many of this broad socioeconomic group turn to populism as a perceived solution to their problems.

DISTRUST OF THE POLITICAL CLASS

The checkered history of the more established political parties—marked as they are by scandals and lacking in credible plans for significant change—has not done anything for the reputation of liberal democracy. In many instances, a loss of confidence in the political establishment has reduced people's previous caution towards embracing more extreme positions on governance. However, they have failed to realize the inherent dangers that populism carries. Many choose to overlook the tragic events of the past and the numerous disasters instigated by populist leaders. Experiences in countries like Venezuela, Argentina, Bangladesh, Pakistan, the Philippines, and South Africa provide illustrative examples. Take the cases of Argentina and Venezuela, where the popular Peronism movement in Argentina and the leadership of former Venezuelan President Hugo Chavez and his successor Nicolás Maduro led to economic decline and instability. Unfortunately, historical amnesia makes people more open to illiberal changes. Fueled by distrust of their country's current leadership, many conclude that breaking democratic norms may be a price worth paying for what they hope will be positive change.

THE INFLUENCE OF SOCIAL MEDIA

If these various developments weren't destabilizing enough, one of the most crucial transformations in the current social landscape is the rise of social media. Social media has become a boon for populist ideas, thanks to the importance placed on algorithmically designed "engagement factors." Advocates of populism have realized (a subject touched upon in Chapter 1) that an exciting lie garners more attention or "engagement" than a boring truth. The algorithms used by social media platforms prioritize sensational ideas (such as conspiracy theories), emotional and direct language, and simplistic slogans.

As a result, these communication devices have become great enablers of populist rhetoric. They allow populist leaders to address their audience directly and provide them with disproportionate coverage. Thus, what populists have realized is that every time they take an extreme position, they receive another invitation to appear in the news, resulting in a narcissistic and very dangerous feedback loop. They know that creating a spectacle will lead to fame, which in turn grants them power, influence, and possibly financial support. Thus, assisted by these social media, these people can shape whatever narrative will capture people's attention, blurring the lines between the ignorant and the informed, between facts and factoids. In other words, social media has proven to be the ideal instrument to mobilize disaffected citizens towards populist, anti-establishment activities by polarizing the public and sowing doubts about democracy.

The internet has led to the formation of a new media landscape, facilitating the production of misinformation and reinforcing echo chambers. It has enabled followers to live in populist bubbles, where they are only exposed to nationalist and xenophobic messages. They learn to distrust fact-based media and evidence-based science. Instead, they feed on conspiracy theories and become suspicious of democratic institutions.

A SEDUCTIVE IDEOLOGY

Populism is undoubtedly fueled by people's sense of political powerlessness. They firmly believe that the world is unjust, and their lack of control leaves them feeling wronged and deprived of what they deserve. In fact, wherever people attribute their perceived vulnerability to external factors beyond their control, populism tends to emerge.

Thus, populists jump at this opportunity, actively feeding into and magnifying this sense of dissatisfaction, wounded national pride, and religious, racial, or ethnic grievances. In fact, perceived threats to a group's cultural identity create a fertile ground for populist and xenophobic reactions and an ideal environment for populist leaders to emerge. These populist demagogues are highly skilled at exploiting people's collective narcissistic injuries by rallying their grievances, fears, and anger.

Certainly, there is nothing wrong with being receptive to the needs of a population—it is, after all, the role of a leader. But when it is used for malicious purposes, benefiting only specific individuals or groups, it can pose a threat to a liberal democracy. Such practices do not bring out the best in people and actively invite human regression. To better understand these regressive processes, we must understand something of the early beginnings of Homo sapiens.

STONE AGE REGRESSIONS

If we analyze the evolutionary history of the human species, we can observe that people have always been inclined towards tribal communalism. In the paleolithic era, our ancestors relied on strong group cohesion as a key component for survival. The fear of various dangers in their environment activated an evolutionary tendency to seek safety in groups. To ensure effective group dynamics, strict collective norms, tight group coordination (fostering a sense of belonging), and an intolerance for deviation were necessary. With the numerous threats they faced, it was essential to draw clear distinctions between friends and enemies. Lengthy discussions were impractical and time-consuming; simplicity and clear direction were needed for survival. As a result, a directive, autocratic form of leadership tended to be favored over complex group dynamics.

Evidently, we have retained some of these Stone Age mental habits. Although these archaic tendencies may be suppressed in contemporary society, it doesn't take much for human beings to regress when under stress. As mentioned repeatedly, when modern human feels threatened, archaic behavior patterns come to the fore, and threats lead to a narrowed cognitive focus, tunnel vision, and often motivate aggression. These will be the occasions when people fall into a dependency mode and ask for authoritative populist leaders to take charge.

Intuitively, populist leaders who rise to the occasion know how to awaken such primal instincts and appeal to the archaic characteristics of the human mind. They recognize the tribal nature of human beings, appealing to their need for belonging and a "chosen" tribe. This sense of belonging provides individuals with a sense of security and explains why the politics of identity can be so attractive.

This archaic heritage helps explain why a rigid collectivist narrative emerges in various populist ideologies—a narrative that depicts a struggle between the favored "in-group" and its enemies. Just as in the past, people may look to a leader for guidance and to help them make the right choices. These psychological dynamics may even raise the question of whether human nature, shaped by evolutionary adaptation, is ill-suited to the psychological requirements of a liberal democracy.

Like our ancient leaders, populist leaders know how to encourage a reversion to more primitive ways of coping with the complexities of the world people inhabit. They exploit people's propensity for tribalism by offering them direction, belonging, status, and significance. They offer their supporters a powerful group identity and a collectivist ideology that provide meaning and personal significance. They do this by oversimplifying and presenting choices in a very stark manner. They effectively create a worldview of "us" versus "them" and portray themselves as clean figures fighting against a corrupt establishment.

Populist leaders further acknowledge that human beings aren't always rational decision-makers. When forced to choose, most people prefer simple explanations for highly complex issues, and this is precisely what populist leaders provide. In the face of threat there is little time for reflection, and the perceived need for action overrules the rational thinking that might ordinarily determine the right approach. Populist leaders use this knowledge to rally their followers, appealing to narcissistic, emotionally charged themes like injustice, betrayal, powerlessness, and victimization—all of which are central concerns of these writings.

GEMEINSCHAFT AND GESELLSCHAFT

Human beings have also had to grapple with the transformation from *Gemeinschaft* (community) to *Gesellschaft* (society).[2] While *Gemeinschaft* is characterized by a strong sense of common identity, shared norms, and close personal relationships, *Gesellschaft* is characterized by impersonal relations, formal organization, and the absence of common, binding norms. As we have transitioned from *Gemeinschaft* to *Gesellschaft*, small social structures such as the family, tribe, or the village—situations where human relationships were prized and the welfare of the entire community took precedence over individual interests—have all but disappeared.

Globalization has turned the planet into an increasingly distant kind of *Gesellschaft* where many people feel disconnected and alienated. The presence of strident individualism, secularism, and the disappearance of intimate interpersonal and group experiences have left people particularly susceptible to the enticing calls of tribal ideologies. Many individuals don't feel they belong anywhere and long for *Gemeinschaft*, the communal social structure of the past.

However, for many people, social media has played a role in creating a pseudo-sense of belonging. These platforms have been effective in establishing substitute, virtual tribes, and populist leaders know how to exploit them to disseminate fake news, conspiracy theories, and sectional group ideologies.

NARCISSISTIC SIGNALING

Populist narratives often emphasize unrecognized greatness and the feeling of being betrayed by adversaries, along with a battle for justice and recognition. The promise of a powerful tribal identity and collectivist ideology seems to give meaning and personal significance to their followers. This appeal is further strengthened by the populist leaders' ability to portray their followers as inherently good and a force of purity and wisdom, in contrast to the evil "others."

This narrative is effective because people like to feel special even through the acknowledgment of illusory virtues and fictitious achievements. These feelings foster a strong identification with the in-group as individuals become increasingly emotionally invested, developing an unrealistic belief in the unparalleled greatness of this virtuous group. In making these statements, populist leaders also tap into the all-too-human quest for perfect happiness.

Such an approach has been used to great effect by populist leaders like Vladimir Putin, Viktor Orbán, Boris Johnson, Jaroslaw Kaczynski, Recep Tayyip Erdoğan, and Narendra Modi. For instance, in Poland, Kaczynski, a religious-nationalist populist, has pushed for a Catholic takeover of the country's institutions from supposed elite secular liberals. In Britain, Brexiteers denounced experts, referred to themselves as "the people," and boasted of smashing the elite. In India, Modi has a long history of denigrating Muslims. By emboldening feelings of collective narcissism, such activities create hypersensitivity to perceived attacks against the in-group. Any kind of behavior is justified as a response to such perceived dangers, as exemplified by the overt actions to overthrow legitimate governments in the United States and Brazil.

MANIPULATING EMOTIONS

The influence of affective states on all aspects of human social behavior extends to political preferences as well. Feelings of anger, fear, disgust, and envy play a crucial role in the appeal of populism. Populist leaders rouse these negative emotions and employ simplistic but emotionally charged messages to captivate their audience. They repeatedly highlight the significance of their own group, using it as a means to construct a positive identity. As mentioned previously, historical leaders like Adolph Hitler, Benito Mussolini, Joseph Stalin, and Mao Zedong were masters of this strategy, while populists such as Orbán in Hungary, Erdoğan in Turkey, and Trump in the United States seem to be following in their footsteps. Their use of primitive identity-based language is evident, often amplified by the power of social media.

Populist leaders like to leverage the psychological dynamics of "feeling wronged" (as discussed in the previous chapters) to mobilize and galvanize political support. In other words, populist attitudes are strongly influenced by the resentment arising from a perceived loss of social status. For this reason, the narratives propagated by populist leaders often cultivate a sense of grievance for past injustices, stoking feelings of anger and demands for retribution among their followers. This explains why populism resonates strongly with citizens who feel disenfranchised and marginalized, even if they belong to a majority ethnic group. They harbor a belief that a "corrupt elite" manipulates its political, economic, and cultural power to serve its own self-interest and enrichment at the expense of the broader populace.

Populist leaders excel at transforming grievances into resentment—a typical emotional reaction to perceived injustices. Often, this sense of being wronged is rooted in nostalgia and longing for a nation's glorified past. These leaders use common narrative features that address grievances and evoke nostalgia for an idealized bygone era. Brexit serves as a prime example of this—a nostalgia for a time when Britain was a global empire. In contrast to liberal democracies, populist narratives are marked by simplicity, a sense of certainty, moral absolutism, group identity, and utopian thinking. They make feelings of being wronged the very purpose of their movement, channeling the desire for justice into a powerful call for political action.

Moreover, populist leaders know how to channel anger towards the current state of affairs into negative partisanship against mainstream political parties. Popular themes include "foreigners are stealing your jobs," "technology favors the wealthy," or "only the little people pay taxes." These kinds of populist narratives are highly effective in fostering emotional identification and creating a distinction between normal people and the elite.

This populist strategy can also contribute to the legitimization of extra-political actions. As mentioned previously, political strategies based on grievances have the potential to escalate conflicts by raising the threshold for what is considered immoral and unacceptable behavior. Unprincipled behavior is fueled when feelings of fear, grievance, and anger give rise to disgust—a powerful emotion that, in our evolutionary past, signaled the presence of contamination and the need for cleansing and elimination. In this regard, disgust can be considered one of the more effective emotions exploited in populist aggression, legitimizing ethnic violence and even genocide by depicting enemies as subhuman contaminants to be eradicated.

The arousal of these various emotional states also creates an empathy gap. While most people tend to feel empathy when they witness the suffering of others, negative labeling diminishes this response when it comes to members of the out-group. This explains why the appeal of populism can bring out the worst in people. Populists often label members of the out-group as an existential threat, constantly emphasizing the dangers faced by the in-group. Inevitably, this process leads to more xenophobia, nationalism, and support for authoritarianism.

CATEGORIZING

Populism exploits the human cognitive tendency to categorize. The act of categorization simplifies reality into extremes. Subsequently, when populists present things in clear-cut categories such as right and wrong or black and white, they tap into the innate human desire for simplicity. Indeed, it is widely acknowledged that without categorization, the world might appear chaotic. Complexity only creates confusion, in which every new experience is seemingly unique and requires extensive interpretation. Populist leaders intuitively grasp how classification acts to simplify and manage the anxiety of the unknown, falsely affirming the intelligence and understanding of a people.

Such categorization goes hand in hand with stereotyping. It encourages individuals to see the world within simplistic black-and-white frameworks, rather than appreciating its subtle shades of gray. This, in turn, fuels another grave danger: dehumanization—a process in which people strip members of the out-group of their fundamental human attributes, including agency, identity, and the ability to experience suffering. In the eyes of the in-group, they are reduced to a subhuman status.

These out-group/in-group dynamics can take many forms. Whether the perceived enemy is cast as the intellectual or political elite of today or the historical industrial elite from the early days of populism, this unifying narrative contributes to the success of populist leaders. A highly skilled and demagogue-like leader, such as Trump, exploits this in-group/out-group categorization to great effect. Such a leader takes advantage of the group identity that his followers seek and confirms their beliefs, allowing their xenophobic tendencies to flourish unchecked.

Populist leaders also know how to exploit the force of confirmation bias referred to earlier, in which people naturally favor and selectively remember information that supports one's preexisting beliefs whilst ignoring contradictory information. Confirmation bias not only reinforces erroneous beliefs but also contributes to the polarization of attitudes. The limited cognitive capacity of individuals, which tends to favor a coherent and integrated belief system, makes confirmation bias highly appealing.

Ironically, poorly informed people tend to overestimate their expertise in making competent judgments. People's inability to recognize their lack of competence is partly due to inflated self-assessment, which is again a mindset often exploited by populist ideologies.

THE PROFILE OF POPULIST LEADERS

Successful populist leaders are usually charismatic individuals who exude self-confidence and certainty and are unwilling to tolerate disagreement. Generally speaking, these autocratic individuals have conventional beliefs about what's right and what's wrong, as well as a strong sense of absolute rectitude regarding their own beliefs and values. This is accompanied by a preference for strong leadership that displays uncompromising power dynamics. They also expect great deference towards those they perceive to be authority figures and can be aggressive towards those who fail to subscribe to their worldview. Furthermore, they prefer simplicity and do not tolerate ambiguity or complex issues. They're also rather impatient in regard to rules and processes, preferring short-cut solutions such as Trump's angry promises to "get things done" or Boris Johnson's more specific mantra to "get Brexit done."

In effect, populist leaders tend to exhibit narcissistic traits while also embodying the psychological and cultural characteristics typical of a country's average voter. By doing so, they facilitate the process of identification between the followers and the leader. Unfortunately, it is the narcissism of these leaders, their apparent unwavering belief in their greatness and the confidence that comes across in their statements, which appears to attract their followers. On closer examination, however, we may discover a very fragile ego underneath, as well as a tendency to project their own feelings of inadequacy, rage, and fear onto a scapegoated group.[3] Furthermore, studying the developmental history of these people, we may discover that they may have experienced a punitive relationship with their parents, particularly having to deal with a strong father figure. Such a background is often associated with the development of authoritarian views later in life.

The more politically extreme a leader's populist orientation is, the more they exhibit these authoritarian qualities. Such leaders radiate certainty and demonstrate consistent, persistent, and uncompromising behavior. Additionally, many possess highly effective oratory skills and know how to use rhetoric to tap into people's psychological needs. They also understand that repetition lends greater credibility to their message, and as a result, they repeat the same message over and over again with conviction and without retraction.

We may have noticed that the communication style of master propagandist Joseph Goebbels has been effectively employed by the likes of Trump, Orbán, Modi, and other populist leaders, whether or not they are consciously aware of it. Similar to the tactics used during the Nazi's Third Reich, these leaders employ populist rhetoric that defines their nations based on faith, race, and ethnicity rather than legal rights. The politicization of anxiety surrounding identity explains why a similar agenda has emerged in country after country. The underlying desire is to defend ethnic hegemony and restore national greatness as a response to the perception of outside threats, particularly globalization. For leaders like France's Marine Le Pen or even Italian Prime Minister Giorgia Meloni, only a select group is considered part of "the people," regardless of their birthplace or citizenship. These populist leaders, above and beyond any institution, embody and represent that group. This is why when populists are in power, any criticism against them will be viewed as an attack on the state itself, leading to critics being labeled enemies of the state or even terrorists. Putin's recent propaganda efforts provide a relevant example of this phenomenon.

PARANOID THINKING

These leaders frequently employ projection as a psychological defense mechanism, projecting onto others what they fear in themselves. However, their self-awareness is very limited, and in their self-constructed world, they always need to be perceived as right. Those who do not share their point of view are labeled as liars. For many populists, their perverse narrative strategy adopts the form of a "big lie," serving to reinforce their self-constructed reality. It is plausible that these individuals feel compelled to lie repeatedly, and they may even begin to believe their own falsehoods. The more implausible and audacious their lies, the less likely their followers are to assume that they have been fabricated. In fact, the bigger the lies, the more persuasive they become.

History reveals that in fascist and Marxist dictatorships, truth has always been secondary to propaganda, and blatant lies often go unchallenged. The same pattern can be observed in the propaganda machine currently operating in Russia. Everything is permissible, regardless of how outrageous the claims may be— whether it is justifying war as a fight against Nazi hegemony in Ukraine or protecting cultural heritage from the godless West. The invocation of moral absolutism and certainty allows these populist, demagogue-like leaders to ignore normal ethical standards and honesty. Surprisingly, many of these populists seem to face limited censorship and consequences even when their dishonesty is exposed, in contrast to what happens to more mainstream leaders.

In many ways, these populist leaders embody the absurdities and fallacies of their movements. Their propagation of "big lies" (often intertwined with conspiracy theories) effectively capitalizes on people's desire to form beliefs based on what is pleasing to imagine, rather than on evidence, rationality, or reality. These conspiracy theories gain credibility as conspirators work in secrecy, withholding access to facts, leading some to assume there must be truth in what is being said. Again, the confirmation bias also plays a role in these conspiracy narratives: People tend to see only what they want to see. This shared worldview becomes a means to bond people and create a shared identity.

Of course, one of the most attractive and recent "big lies" associated with a number of conspiracy theories has been Trump's assertion that he won the US presidential election, despite all evidence to the contrary. However, history is full of instances of individuals embracing bizarre and unfounded beliefs. The medieval witch trials, religious wars, mass delusions, belief in human sacrifice, paranormal beliefs, and the QAnon cult are all examples that demonstrate the power of confirmation bias. Among the conspiracy theories, we can observe the enduring persistence of ideas about Jewish conspiracies, which were recently revived by Hungary's Orbán, who accused the philanthropist George Soros of leading a financiers' conspiracy to manipulate the EU and subjugate Hungary. It is evident that populist movements take advantage of the human tendency for gullibility by disregarding the truth, thus giving their narratives an undeserved advantage in shaping political attitudes.

But what can be done to prevent the ascent of populist movements and protect liberal democracies? Regardless of the actions taken, democracy will never be an easy form of government, as it is a continuously evolving system. As the French political philosopher Alexis de Tocqueville aptly stated, "Agitation and mutability are inherent in the nature of democratic republics, just as stagnation and sleepiness are the law of absolute monarchies."[4]

NOTES

[1] Obama's Speech; McCain's Palinomy (2008, August 30–31). http://www.counterpunch.org/cockburn08302008.html CounterPunch

[2] Ferdinand Tönnies (1887). *Gemeinschaft und Gesellschaft*. Leipzig: Fues's Verlag.

[3] Theodor Adorno, Else Frenkel-Brunswik, Daniel J. Levinson, and R. Nevitt Sanford (1950). *The Authoritarian Personality*. New York: Harper & Brothers.

[4] Alexis de Tocqueville (1835). *Democracy in America*, Volume 1. Google Books, p. 399.

6

ANTI-DEMAGOGUERY

The demagogue is one who preaches doctrines he knows to be untrue to men he knows to be idiots.

—Henry L. Mencken

Democracy is four wolves and a lamb voting on what to have for lunch.

—Ambrose Bierce

LIBERAL DEMOCRACY: A FRAGILE SYSTEM

As suggested in the previous chapter, cultural and socioeconomic factors play an important role in fueling populism. What has also become clear, however, is that the emotional politics of identity are often more powerful than the rational politics of economic interests. Populism succeeds because it thrives on creating dark narratives that provide "tribal" comforts, playing on people's cognitive limitations in order to fire up their emotions. Although economics are crucial, support for populism is strongly influenced

DOI: 10.4324/9781003427117-7

by cultural elements. Populist narratives gain traction by employing utopistic and messianic ideas, promising a perfect future that justifies every sacrifice and gives meaning and significance to followers. For instance, the promises of a "Thousand-Year Reich" (Nazism) or a communist utopia (Marxism) had powerful appeal and fostered robust social bonds. In comparison, liberal ideologies struggle to compete with these more messianic messages.

Frankly speaking, a liberal democracy is a very fragile system that requires thoughtful and rational consideration, as well as strict adherence to its delicate norms. These norms include tolerance of different opinions, free speech, and a commitment to a rule-based framework. Democracy demands a willingness to grant space to people with whom you may disagree. In contrast, demagogic, populist leaders effortlessly exploit the inherent human inclination for simplified, tribal thinking and intergroup animosity.

Liberal politicians need to acknowledge that the scope and magnitude of societal change are among its major challenges as a cause of significant anxiety among populations. Many people have serious—and entirely justified—financial concerns. Economic progress in recent decades has disproportionately benefited a small elite, evident in the outrageous financial packages awarded to top executives. Populist leaders have astutely exploited this growing anxiety to gain electoral advantage, assuring their audiences that they're willing to do what is necessary to fix the problems. In essence, the rise of populist parties can be viewed as the result of protest votes by people who feel unheard and ignored.

There is always the danger of complacency when liberal actors have been in power for some time, as they may have become disconnected from their constituencies. Bureaupathology, or "red-tape syndrome," can render leaders unresponsive to the needs of the public. Therefore, it is important for them to recognize populism as the rejection of a distant, technocratic, and increasingly irrelevant ruling political elite whose messages no longer resonate with the majority of people. Such passivity generates frustration and contempt from certain segments of the electorate, creating an ideal environment for demagogue politicians to fill the vacuum with simplistic populist rhetoric, hatred of the opposition, and a proliferation of untruths.

GOVERNMENTS—GET IN TOUCH WITH YOUR PEOPLE

A major challenge for mainstream democratic leaders is to prevent such an estrangement with the populace. They need to revitalize grassroots mobilization if they are to thwart populist attempts to exploit any potential disconnect between citizens and their political parties. Advocates of liberal democracy should foster regular and meaningful interactions between diverse groups of constituents at the community level. These interactions can diminish prejudice, challenge perceptions of threat, and improve levels of tolerance.

If these advocates demonstrate a greater responsiveness to the concerns of the general public, they will also have the opportunity to point out that populists lack significant experience in governing a country. In fact, they should emphasize that these individuals disdain the normal operations of government, try to overthrow political institutions, and are willing to block democratic processes. They should also make it clear to their constituencies that populists possess limited knowledge about public affairs and only know how to present simplistic slogans. Alongside these efforts to highlight the limitations of populist leaders, they should never underestimate their allure. Even though they may lack experience, their supporters often see them as untarnished by the mistakes made by mainstream parties, mistakes that will almost certainly be exploited by their opponents.

What also needs to be pointed out is that populists are often masters of nihilism and negativity. Furthermore, they excel in the politics of personality, creating a political movement centered purely around the promotion of their own beliefs and interests. They play to their constituents and to the nation with sweeping claims and broad denials, personal attacks on the opposition, and a willingness to undermine the core tenets of democracy, all with a sense of joyful exuberance at the damage that may be done. Rather than offering constructive proposals, they create a climate of fear, anger, and distrust.

Still, despite the lack of substance in their arguments, it doesn't take much to sway a population towards the populist agenda. Whatever tactics these populists employ, it is crucial for establishment figures to take them seriously. History has repeatedly shown that if these populists have their way, liberal democracy as we know it may be endangered.

Consequently, supporters of liberal democracy face a significant challenge in building trust, in terms of both gaining the electorate's confidence in their elected officials and fostering trust in the democratic institutions. This involves finding ways to provide greater representation for those who feel disenfranchised, which may include the use of referenda—Switzerland being a good example of a country that embraces this approach to stay attuned to its constituencies. Such measures reassure people that their concerns are being taken seriously. It is also vital to recognize the specific policy needs of marginalized groups and acknowledge that some members of society do not enjoy the same advantages that others enjoy. This initial step can help prevent populism from gaining momentum.

THE JAPANESE EXAMPLE

A radical solution to ward off populism could be to follow the example of the Japanese. Consciously or unconsciously, they have held populism at bay through economic and other interventions. Their governments have been able to slow down the negative effects of globalization by using measures such as high tariffs to protect domestic producers, particularly in agriculture. In addition, Japan, compared to other countries, has much less income inequality. High inheritance taxes and comparatively lower executive pay (compared to most Western countries) make Japan a much more egalitarian society compared to other advanced economies.

Furthermore, Japanese governments have significantly restricted immigration, making it extremely difficult to become a Japanese citizen. In addition, forces that typically drive change in other countries, such as the empowerment of women and minorities—factors that often foster support for populism among those who fear a loss of status—have had minimal impact on Japanese society. As a result, the Japanese voting public has little reason to blame foreigners or special interest groups for potential economic woes. Identity politics centered on class, religious, or ethnic differences do not play a substantial role in their elections.

Furthermore, the Japanese mainstream media shuns sensationalism and is much more inclined to support the status quo. Japanese journalists often maintain friendly relations with government figures, denying populists the kind of publicity that would greatly benefit politicians like Boris Johnson, Jair Bolsonaro, or Donald Trump. But while Japan's approach to countering populism is intriguing, it may not be the simplest or most suitable example to emulate. Different countervailing measures need to be taken.

A BROADER PERSPECTIVE

Leaders with a more liberal democratic outlook should address voter anxiety by presenting policy solutions that align with society's extended vision for the future. To demonstrate foresight, they should place proposed policies within a broader narrative about the country, offering achievable calls to action for the target audience. Here, they can benefit from highlighting common, unifying beliefs, practices, processes, and institutions while stressing the fundamental values that shaped the country's identity today. Adopting such a broad perspective will make it more likely that these stories stick. In other words, they should seek to create unifying and aspirational narratives, be intentional about mythbusting, highlight solutions, and emphasize their effectiveness in getting things done.

Furthermore, it is essential to bear in mind that even though populist leaders frame issues as urgent crises, they rarely provide solutions to address those problems. Advocates of liberal democracy must therefore convey to their constituencies that the populist tendency to merely diagnose the problem and make sweeping, simplistic generalizations is insufficient. They should point out that their claims, including personal attacks on opponents, do not lead to progress. They should make quite clear—emphasizing to the general public—that what's needed are solution-based approaches to address the challenges at hand.

When presenting their vision for the future, champions of liberal democracy should also refrain from simply reacting to the agenda put forth by populists. It is necessary to avoid linking racial, ethnic, and religious identities with partisan affiliation, thus avoiding the tendency to view politics solely through the lens of identity. Instead of engaging with the dark, divisive, and polarizing narratives of populists, they should address their country's challenges. They must recognize that their choice of words and their talents at framing will play a critical role in countering the sweeping statements of populism. By creating a distinct and nuanced discourse, they can reiterate that a leader's challenge is to provide robust solutions.

AN EDUCATIONAL STAND

For many populist movements, national sovereignty appears to be the utmost priority. It serves as an important argument when they advocate for handing power back to the people. As a result, most populist parties harbor distrust towards international rules and tend to adopt aggressive "zero-sum" foreign policies. There seems to be a nostalgic longing for a mythical "golden age" when protective national states held sway, as exemplified by the Brexit case. However, this obsession with national sovereignty also means that populist parties lack convincing solutions to the challenges of the 21st century. Many of the major present issues are inherently transnational in character, such as climate change, migration, economic development, scientific and technological progress, and regional and global stability. Supporters of liberal democracy should emphasize that none of these objectives can be achieved by embracing a siege mentality. On the contrary, it requires international engagement and cooperation.

However, rational arguments often hold limited sway over "true believers." Despite the resistance from these individuals, leaders should strive to present their point of view in a repetitive, simple, and easily understandable way. As populists have discovered, such narratives are more likely to resonate and leave a lasting impact.

If supporters of liberal democracy present their ideas clearly, simply, and with conviction, populists will find it more difficult to make inroads. When people understand the underlying reasons for specific actions, there is a greater degree of acceptance. Unfortunately, mainstream parties often use overly complicated language to convey their messages and would be far more effective if they used simpler campaign strategies. In comparison, populists tend to employ a more emotional and instinctual approach to politics, making them better at direct messaging and providing people with a transcendental experience. Champions of liberal democracy would do well to learn from their example.

In addition, advocates of liberal democracy need to take on an educational role and be responsive to voter concerns about economic and cultural factors, while underlining the importance of democratic principles to ensure a country's success. They should reiterate that strong cultural norms are the safeguards of democracy, with a crucial aspect being the acceptance of diverse points of view. By taking an educational approach, they can enhance their audience's understanding of social issues and help people identify solutions that weren't apparent to them before. Consequently, people may become more willing to support these proposed solutions.

By adopting this approach, those committed to liberal democracy can reduce people's susceptibility to the unrealistic promises of populist leaders. Through effective communication of their ideas in a clear and articulate manner, their audiences will be less likely to dismiss any criticism of their policy positions and more inclined to uphold the principles of democratic governance.

FACTS VERSUS FACTOIDS

Leaders of liberal democracies may be tempted to point out the lies propagated by populist leaders; however, this strategy doesn't seem to be very effective. Presenting people with "the facts" or attempting to break down echo chambers by presenting opposing views only tends to exacerbate polarization. In fact, the more they highlight the framing and rhetoric of populist leaders, the more they will allow their opponents' ideas to dominate the political dialogue. This tactic legitimizes and amplifies the often-outrageous narratives put forth by populists and compromises the underlying principles of tolerance and pluralism. Mainstream parties that adopt the language of populists not only damage their credibility but also alienate core groups of voters, leading to weaker performance at the ballot box. Instead, advocates of liberal democracy should appeal to values—enduring beliefs that shape individuals' attitudes and behavior—that resonate with their target audiences. By speaking to these values, they can tap into the higher-level reasoning of their audience, making their message more salient and persuasive.

While it may be tempting to blame populist leaders for their lies, it is worth remembering that blame is central to the populist rhetoric. Populists frame the challenges faced by "the people" as the consequence of a corrupt and incompetent establishment. They believe that blaming the elite or selected groups, such as immigrants, for societal ills, will be an effective means of gaining attention and support. When individuals with a more liberal outlook join this blame game, it only heightens polarization and reinforces the populist notion of a "corrupt elite," thereby fueling the momentum of these populist narratives.

This doesn't mean, however, that liberal democratic actors should keep silent when populists spew inaccuracies and conspiracy theories. If an outrageous lie necessitates a response, it is wise to resist a knee-jerk reaction and actively exercise a degree of caution. Refutations should be done sparingly and are more effective if made in close temporal proximity to the initial case of misinformation. They should set the record straight and provide an alternative story to help fill in the resulting gap, allowing those embracing populist views to understand why false "facts" need to be discarded.

THE POWER OF POSITIVITY

As mentioned before, social media's algorithms mean the pessimism of populists has a willing audience. As doomsday artists, they tell anyone willing to listen that they're being conned and betrayed, arguing that governments declare one thing and then do precisely the opposite, often to further interests unrelated to the issue at hand. According to these populists, life has become increasingly precarious, the economy is going down the drain, and moral and social relations are worsening. But it is worth questioning whether their vision is a realistic summary of a country's situation, as conditions often aren't as dire as portrayed and there is room for hope in the future.

Therefore, it is up to advocates of liberal democracy to counter these doomsday scenarios. Instead of echoing populists' delusional statements, they should harness the power of positivity and make a concerted effort to reframe the doomsday scenarios into more constructive, positive alternatives.

In rebalancing these accusations, they should be realistic and acknowledge that not everything is positive for everyone. However, they should also highlight the potential for improvement, efforts to reduce economic inequality, and the creation of new employment opportunities. To avoid it becoming an exercise in wishful thinking, they should present realistic proposals for how these changes can be achieved.

But it is also critical to convey that things will be different from the past. Liberal democratic leaders need to be forthright about the impact of globalization and new technologies on specific industries and jobs. However, they should explain that these developments will elevate the quality of life for society as a whole, even if certain segments of the population will be negatively affected in the short term. Honesty is essential, including acknowledging that not everyone's standard of living will keep on rising, and some people's net income may remain stagnant. In addition, it is vital to emphasize that animosity towards outsiders or foreigners will not solve their problems. As mentioned before, adopting a siege mentality towards the outside world and condemning globalism and technological advances isn't the answer. Consequently, a good starting point for discussing the benefits of a liberal democracy is to present a realistic picture without glossing over the challenges. This approach will also be instrumental in warding off the dangers of populism.

Liberal democratic leaders must also stress that relying on past glory is not a viable option. Instead, they need to offer an inclusive, ambitious political vision for the future that benefits all citizens. In their vision of a globalized world, they should specify the public services to be provided and outline plans for improving living conditions. This includes identifying potential job creation opportunities, determining feasible and advantageous industry specializations, and outlining the attainable abilities and education levels for the younger generation.

INCLUSION

Ironically, one approach to counter populism is through inclusion. The idea is that in allowing populist parties entry into a parliamentary system, they may moderate their extreme views. This can be seen as a form of socialization with the aim of encouraging populists to accept a liberal democratic system. After all, populism is inherently hostile to traditional political processes and the values commonly associated with constitutionalism, such as the constraints on the will of the majority, checks and balances, protections for minorities, and even fundamental human rights. Thus, being part of such a system could be a great learning experience for these individuals. Of course, this path should be pursued with great care, as there is always a risk of derailment. There is always the possibility that this experiment will fail, leading to populist actors contaminating democracy. As populists are prone to promoting division over unity, they may use this opportunity to obstruct democratic processes, as tragically demonstrated by the rise of Nazis and Marxists to power.

STOP DANCING WITH THE DEVIL

Engaging with populists can be likened to dancing with the devil. It has a tantalizing allure, even though the dancers ultimately end up in perilous situations. The philosopher Bertrand Russell once posed the question: "Why is propaganda so much more successful when it stirs up hatred than when it tries to stir up friendly feeling?" The fact that so many populist leaders have been shameless liars reflects not only on them but also on the people who believe in them. Perhaps the catalyst for populism lies as much in the followers as in the ideas and characters of the populist leaders that ignite them. As populists have discovered, when the people want the impossible, only dishonesty can satisfy their demands. To quote Aristotle, "Before a crowd, the ignorant are more persuasive than the educated."

As previously mentioned, populism can be perceived as a form of human regression. Unfortunately, history has repeatedly demonstrated how humanity's inclination to regress poses great risks to our world. Human beings easily revert to behaviors reminiscent of paleolithic times, where tribalism, autocracy, scapegoating, and zero-sum thinking were commonplace. These regressive behavior patterns not only manifest as psychological forms of regression but can also take on a sociocultural form, urging a return to long-gone eras.

Populists also disregard the importance of accumulated knowledge that can advance human progress. They look down on innovation as ideas presented by "elites" and "experts" and reject the philosophical ideas of the Enlightenment, including liberal democratic principles like freedom of speech and diversity of opinion. Instead, take an anti-rational stand, neglecting to advocate reason or logical thinking. According to populist demagogue Adolf Hitler, "If you wish the sympathy of the broad masses, you must tell them the crudest and most stupid things." Vladimir Putin clearly concurs, as evidenced by his comment, "As a rule, [populism] is done for the sake of political expediency by those who do not care about the consequences, who do not think even one step ahead, who do not want to think and do not intend to honor their commitments."[1] He certainly seems to know what he is talking about.

The advocates of populism, however, tend to overlook the inherent limitations of human nature and the dangers posed by human fallibility. Even though autocrats can act quickly and decisively, they are also susceptible to making huge mistakes, as nobody is willing to challenge them when they're wrong. Notable examples include the recent missteps of Xi Jinping concerning Covid-19, Vladimir Putin's "special military operation," and Recep Tayyip Erdoğan's economical machinations and his response to the devastating earthquake. Their flawed decisions are the result of living in echo chambers, where their subordinates only tell them what they want to hear. They tend to dismiss rule-governed institutions and constitutional checks and balances that constrain the power of imperfect human beings. Instead, they adhere to the belief that furthering their cause requires increasing authoritarianism, driven by a dogmatic fundamentalist ideology.

When populist leaders present themselves as defenders of liberty, it is essential to judge them by what they do, not what they preach. It is clear that these leaders are rarely genuinely interested in solving people's problems; instead, their primary concern is serving their own interests. In the United States, for instance, many Republicans seem to be more interested in entering politics to become celebrities rather than to pass legislation. They have learned that the more outrageous they behave, the more attention they garner, and the easier it becomes to attract funds for their causes. Countries led by these kinds of people typically evolve into predatory, superstitious, and divided societies rather than civilized, reasonable, and united ones.

The tragic irony of populists is that, when they come into power, they often resort to the very sins they once criticized in the "corrupt elites." They end up taking away the rights of the citizens, just like they accused the elites of doing. Often, they see themselves as the embodiment of the state, contrary to their promises of dismantling the establishment and "draining the swamp." Hence, it is delusional to think that populists can improve our democracies. In the end, populists are merely a different form of elite, seeking power through the collective fantasy of political purity.

However, as mentioned before, supporters of liberal democracy should be careful not to label populism as merely a pathology of the simple-minded masses, dismissing the will of the people as backward, primitive, and problematic. Rather, they should listen to their complaints and take notice. A populist movement has the potential to alter the dynamics of political debate by bringing attention to issues that many people care about but have been overlooked by the political establishment. Advocates of liberal democracy should acknowledge that democracies can grow stale and may require reform. Thus, despite the negative attributes, it is fair to say that populism can sometimes have a positive effect on liberal democracy.

THE END OF HISTORY

After World War II, many believed that a new era had dawned and that the unfortunate war would be the last of its kind. There was hope that, given the horror of it all, religious oppression and rampant nationalism would become a thing of the past, and populism would lose its appeal. Autocrats and despots had their day in the sun, and the future appeared promising for liberal democracy. How could we all have been so naïve? Despite discrediting all the brutal movements of the 20th century, from fascism to communism, we have witnessed new autocracies rising from the ashes. It highlights what a fragile construction democratic governance really is—akin to a utopian concept that can easily self-destruct.

In light of the ongoing success of many populist leaders, it seems that humans tend to suffer from a severe case of collective amnesia. Memories of past atrocities instigated by such leaders have quickly faded all. Another contributing factor could be the willingness of many individuals to exchange personal freedom for the promise of material security and domestic safety. Moreover, humans have proven to be far too gullible, meaning that old battles may have to be fought again to maintain truth, memory, and freedom.

Given the dangers of populism, all of us have a responsibility to resist the first signs of its emergence. What needs to be kept in mind is that remaining silent, passive, and taking no action is itself a form of action. When the warning signs become apparent, we must speak up and defend the truth. As Martin Niemöller, a prominent Lutheran German pastor, once said in reference to the Nazi regime:

> First, they came for the socialists, and I did not speak out—because I was not a socialist.
>
> Then they came for the trade unionists, and I did not speak out—because I was not a trade unionist.
>
> Then they came for the Jews, and I did not speak out—because I was not a Jew.
>
> Then they came for me—and there was no one left to speak for me.

We should always be on guard for dictatorships, seductive as their songs may be. But perhaps Sacha Baron Cohen has it right when the protagonist in the film *The Dictator* said:

> Why are you guys so anti-dictators? Imagine if America was a dictatorship. You could let 1% of the people have all the nation's wealth. You could help your rich friends get richer by cutting their taxes. And bailing them out when they gamble and lose. You could ignore the needs of the poor for health care and education. Your media would appear free but would secretly be controlled by one person and his family. You could wiretap phones. You could torture foreign prisoners. You could have rigged elections. You could lie about why you go to war. You could fill your prisons with one particular racial group, and no one would complain. You could use the media to scare the people into supporting policies that are against their interests.

NOTE

[1] Interview by Vladimir Putin to Nippon TV and Yomiuri Newspaper (2016, December 13). *President of Russia*. http://en.kremlin.ru/events/president/news/53455

7

DO DICTATORSHIPS DESERVE SUCH A BAD RAP?

History proves that all dictatorships, all authoritarian forms of government are transient. Only democratic systems are not transient. Whatever the shortcomings, mankind has not devised anything superior.

—Vladimir Putin

If you were to ask me whether you need a dictatorship to run India, No, you do not. Whether you need a powerful person who believes in concentrating power, No, you do not. If you were to ask me to choose between democratic values and wealth, power, prosperity and fame, I will very easily and without any doubt choose democratic values.

—Narendra Modi

Would you want to be a dictator? To have absolute power, limitless economic opportunity, and the ability to get rid of people you don't like? Wouldn't it be great to be at the center of everything,

DOI: 10.4324/9781003427117-8

to have everybody at your beck and call? Surely, this is an ideal way to feel good about yourself. In fact, on paper, being a dictator looks to be a great experience. And if you're family oriented, who knows, you could even turn a dictatorship into a family business with a son or daughter to follow in your footsteps. Just look at North Korea. Is it not incredible that the family business is now in its third generation? They really know how to overcome the "rags to riches" scenario over the course of three generations. As a family firm, they are the envy of the world. To all intents and purposes, its present leader, Kim Jong Un, should be viewed as a role model for all dictators. If you were to take a hard look at the situation, you would see a person of great foresight. Look at the skill with which he has been running his nuclear weapons program; what more fantastic way to invest in the future of this family firm?

Given these displays of greatness, why behave in more democratic ways? Isn't it a fact that democracies stand only for much talk but very little action? Adding to democracy's negative image is its volatility, evident in an ever-changing parade of political actors. Clearly, it is a system that's totally unstable.

Of course, there are always killjoys, those people who argue that, in dictatorships, hubris will be their weak link. They suggest that dictators easily become too full of themselves and stop listening to others. These spoilsports argue that dictators can become too narcissistic, with disastrous consequences. But if so, what's really the problem? I should know, shouldn't I? Don't we all have an ego?

And what is it that is so wrong with a bit of narcissism? Consider carefully how it promotes mental toughness and focused leadership. Aren't these the exact qualities people want, confused as most of them always seem to be? From what I have seen, people want to be led by those willing to take a stand, leaders who are prepared to attend to people's basic needs, leaving them free to do other things.

A DIY DICTATORSHIP

What few realize is that dictators can make people truly feel free. These exact words were spoken by the late dictator of Cuba, Fidel

Castro—a man who really knew how to liberate and give hope to his people. Very much like him, I too have been a true liberator of people. In fact, following his example and speaking of hope and promise is how I got to where I am now. Like him, I have told all those are willing to listen that I represent the national will. What has helped me in my journey is that most people, though they may pretend to be opposed to dictatorships, are quite willing to allow their minds and ways of life to be twisted. In this respect, I have always appreciated the statement of the Greek storyteller Aesop, who said, "Those who voluntarily put power into the hands of a tyrant . . . must not wonder if it be at last turned against themselves." How true that when liberty exceeds intelligence, it begets chaos, which begets dictatorship. Such a nice equation!

LAY THE GROUNDWORK

Of course, to make a dictatorship palatable, you need to lay the groundwork. What I have learned from experience is that however you go about it, it is better to do so in a relatively quiet manner. The aspiring dictator should not overdo it—not at first at least, but play your cards well and be patient. Take my example: I started by pretending that I was supporting existing laws, knowing that when I had the power, I would later destroy them.

BIDE YOUR TIME

Do not rock the boat too much or too early. You never know whether you might upset some high-minded people who may later plot against you. No, to transform a more democratic form of government into some sort of autocracy, it is better to go slowly. Bear in mind that it may take some time before people will see things your way, so be patient. Even though you may be eager to set the gears of your ego in motion, it is better to do so subtly. In other words, you need to be perceptive enough to know when the time is right to crank those gears into overdrive.

MAKE LIKE YOU'RE A MAN OF THE PEOPLE

If I were to give you another piece of advice on your journey to power, it would be to be smart and show some humility. You need to convince the populace that you're really a man of the people. As Joseph Goebbels, Hitler's minister of propaganda, said so pointedly, "Whoever can conquer the street will one day conquer the state, for every form of power politics and any dictatorship-run state has its roots in the street." And while you pretend to be a man of the people, make it equally clear that you stand for stability. Remember that people hate uncertainty. In fact, when the people of a country have to choose between anarchy and dictatorship, they will always choose the latter. To most people, times of trouble are unsettling, and anarchy comes to be viewed as the worst form of dictatorship.

THE INSTALLMENT PLAN

Look at the world's greatest dictators and notice that all have established their reign in a gradual manner. And as we speak, we can observe leaders like Viktor Orbán, Recep Erdoğan, Narendra Modi, and Benjamin Netanyahu practicing this approach to impressive effect. Perhaps the greatest current role model for this way of changing governmental practices has been Vladimir Putin. Many continue to marvel at how he has managed to change Russia into a solid dictatorship. He did this on an installment plan basis, step by little step.

I also got where I am now on just such an installment plan basis. To attain my present position, I had to play my cards very carefully. Initially, I preached to all and sundry that I was an advocate of more democratic governmental practices; I told the people that I was looking out for all of their needs. Of course, this was merely a matter of speech. After all, you cannot take care of or please everybody.

Looking back, some people are amazed to realize that their country has come to be led by a more "directive" form of government. Only with hindsight do they see that what they thought was going to be a democracy has turned into something very different. I find it sad, however, that some people are unable to recognize this as a happy ending. Obviously, they don't know what's good for them. But even though some people may need more convincing than others, I remain confident that, given time, they will see the present form of government to be what it is—something that is good for everybody.

GOOD RIDDANCE TO SKEPTICS

Some of these malcontents, negative as they seem to be, claim that the story and circumstances that are the making of a dictatorship are always the same. According to them, it begins with leaders who pretend to be enlightened; they allege that they're going to deliver the populace from their bondage; they tell people that they're saving them from past humiliations. They will right the wrongs. What these skeptics also say is that if *they* were in charge, they would establish justice, freedom, and peace.

This is the exact script that a talented dictator like Daniel Ortega of Nicaragua has been pursuing. After overthrowing the previous dictator—saying to the people that he was liberating them—he is now doing an impressive job, following exactly in his predecessor's very footsteps. It is just unfortunate that so many people can't appreciate the great things he is now doing for his country. Wisely, more than a hundred thousand of these troublemakers have now left the country, and frankly I think "good riddance!"

Clearly, people who are concerned about dictatorships need to have their heads examined. They fail to realize what's good for them or grasp the idea that dictatorships are fantastic forms of government. As a dictator myself, I really know what I am talking about and have the conviction that my way is the way all leaders should run a country. In fact, most of the people I ask how they feel about the merits of a strong-person rule appear happy to agree with me. And to tell you the truth, I find it quite endearing that they realize what's good for them and have come to see that my ideas are for the betterment of all. I know that people who see things in a more holistic manner realize that the rights of the individual aren't so important, nor is protecting them in the best interest of the nation.

THE SIMPLER LIFE IS TO AGREE

Frankly speaking, it is important that people agree with me. Life becomes so much simpler when everyone does what I tell them to do. Fortunately for me and most dictators, people are "sheeples" at heart; most do what they are told. What I have also discovered is that most people don't *like* to think for themselves. It is testament to basic human nature how easily people get used to a dictatorship. Looking around today, most of the people whom I meet seem to love the way I run the country; they love their servitude; they like to be at my beck and call. Admittedly, I am easily upset to hear remarks that suggest the people in my country are now living in a subtle, not too painful, concentration camp.

Given the mostly positive reactions to my government, I find it hard to understand the statement of Lord Acton when he says that too much power corrupts both the heart and the mind. How wrong can you be to think that having unlimited power will be dangerous? How misguided can you be to argue that there is a possible Caligula in even the gentlest of human souls? To compare me with a Caligula shows how wrong people can be; it is much more accurate to say that I am saving people from themselves. I am rescuing people from their existential aloneness, their anxieties, their responsibility to think, and their reluctance to make decisions. Truth be told, I am actually inspiring hope and meaning in order to counteract people's sense of despair and lack of life's purpose. Without me, I am sure that most of my subjects would feel totally lost and bewildered. In fact, my way of running the country is actually simplifying their lives. I hope that my people know that life is much less complicated under a dictatorship.

ENJOYING THE SIMPLER LIFE

I am pleased to point out that people in my country no longer need to waste their time on voting, especially since I'm making sure that the outcome will be guaranteed. Still, I am kind enough to let those who want to vote go through the motions. Plus, it is always nice to hear that 99 percent of the populace stands behind you. Of course, I make sure that the elections are very well managed; I am not in the business of allowing elections that could remove me from my position! Here again, I have taken Putin as my role model. How admirable to see that on the first day in office, he introduced legislation that reformed and over five years effectively dismantled the Russian electoral system. I hope his people now appreciate the fact that anything that passes for elections in Russia has nothing to do with actual elections. It is more like a pipedream, a hallucination. Clearly, Putin always knew what was good for the country. Like me, he has really been a savior of his people.

History has been full of saviors like Putin and me. Over the centuries, so many dictators have made their populace proud, the kinds of leaders who filled their subjects with admiration. And I am very much like them. I have been doing so many great things to make my people happy. The writer Aldous Huxley could not be more wrong when he said, "So long as men worship the Caesars and Napoleons, Caesars and Napoleons will duly rise and make them miserable." Think instead of the pharaohs of Egypt, Nebuchadnezzar of Babylon, Darius of Persia, Cyrus the Great, Alexander the Great, Julius Caesar, Hannibal, Genghis Khan, Tamerlane, Attila the Hun, Napoleon Bonaparte, Adolph Hitler, Mao, and Stalin. All of them were great people who made an incredible mark on history. Clearly, all of them were welcomed with great cheer by their subjects. Their fantastic efforts transformed their societies for the better. Yet still, there remain these killjoys who suggest the history of mankind to be one of subjugation and exploitation of a great majority of people by an elite few. How can people be so misguided? Don't they have any brains?

WHO DOESN'T HAVE AN INNER DESPOT?

Even though I envisage myself as an enlightened dictator, I don't think that there is anything wrong with prioritizing my own interests above those of others. After all, we all need to look out for number one—who else is otherwise going to do it? Further still, why should looking out for number one not be beneficial to other people? It could become a great win-win situation. People who don't realize this, I call hypocrites, for I am quite sure given the same opportunity, they would act similarly. The English writer Daniel Defoe said, "All men would be tyrants if they could." So, why should I be different? I merely took advantage of the opportunity given to me to become what most people desire to be. I am just actualizing people's inner despot.

Keeping this characteristic of human nature in mind, who needs prattle about democratic values, respect for human rights, equality, and inclusivity? Democracies, as we know, are far from being perfect. They are prone to every error, from incompetence and corruption to complete gridlock. In fact, it has always surprised me how willing people are to submit themselves to the collective wisdom of an imperfect and frequently disengaged public. As I have said before, most people tend to be like sheeples. They follow the leader. I strongly believe that no competent dictator would show more stupidity than what's called the voice of the majority in a democracy.

Isn't it also true that there could exist much more cultural and spiritual freedom under autocratic rule than would be the case in many a democracy? In fact, it is quite conceivable that a democratic government with a doctrinaire majority is going to be more autocratic than a dictatorship. Whilst under a democracy, I think that the era of individualism, liberalism, humanitarianism, and freedom is fast coming to its end. From what I know about human nature, it is much better when people are protected from themselves. That, in fact, is true freedom. After all, you need the freedom to kill freedom.

Knowing all this, I find it very sad to hear that some people still don't appreciate the good things dictators are doing for their countries. Those prepared to invest some time in evaluating dictatorships would likely conclude that it makes for a much more effective form of government. Just think of Lee Kuan Yew, the late prime minister of Singapore. In his three-decade rule, he transformed an underdeveloped city state with no natural resources, constrained by a very limited land area and small army, into a shining example of a developed country. Still, despite all the good things he did for his country, how depressing that some deranged souls have been complaining about his autocratic measures, which included reducing the influence of the press, outlawing protests, and, at times, arbitrarily detaining people. Incredibly enough, he has also been accused—given the alleged desire to consolidate his power—of weakening independent institutions such as the judiciary and legislative bodies. Nevertheless, I stand by my opinion that the dictatorship of the few, compared to the initiative of the millions, can produce a much happier and more prosperous society. It is for all to see how very messy democracies tend to be.

ACCOUNTABILITY (IN THEORY)

Unfortunately, I know that there will always be grumblers, people who aren't prepared to accept that I'm doing really good, when in fact I am a true servant of the people. I strongly believe that concentrating power in the hands of a single person is the best way to steer the population of a country. It is the way to provide them with a sense of direction. And I don't believe all these spoilsports who say that it leads to the suppression of political opposition— that for a country's citizens, it comes with a restriction on free speech, censorship, and limited or no political participation. Not only do they exaggerate, but they also make too much of such trivial matters. In addition, I think that they're also very wrong when they question problems with accountability. How negative can people be?

Everyone knows that I am accountable. I always allow for complaints that I deem to be reasonable. And what's more, I will continue to take great care even of those who make unreasonable complaints. I make sure that everybody is listened to, even if some of these complainers may be in store for a surprise. At the danger of repeating myself, people who argue that the absence of basic civil liberties undermines human rights are out of their minds. People should be more trusting of me. Haven't I always been a man of the people? In everything I do, I have always taken the people's best interest at heart.

Also, I don't agree with the suggestion that my autocratic system of government will soon degenerate—that it brings out the worst in people. What nonsense to suggest that using coercive force always attracts people of low morality! I have even heard people say that dictators will always surround themselves with scoundrels. How could they? Clearly, these people have the facts completely wrong. The like-minded people that I have carefully chosen to help me run the government aren't scoundrels at all. Like me, they're high-minded. They have to be, considering how supportive they are of my ideas. What's wrong with being supported by people who agree with you? It makes any decision-making process so much simpler.

THE CORRUPTION CRITICS

A related accusation that I have heard is that corruption can become endemic in dictatorships. People who have the nerve to say so reason that when power is concentrated, there will be fewer checks and balances. They argue that dictatorships lack independent institutions such as a free press, an impartial judiciary, and effective anti-corruption agencies—the kinds of civil institutions that promote transparency, accountability, and the rule of law. Some who don't like my way of governing even go as far as to say that an absence of these checks and balances will only enable the unchecked abuse of power. According to these killjoys, countries that operate under these conditions create patronage networks and even imply that I would be tempted to distribute favors, privileges, and resources to my loyal supporters in exchange for their political support. Continuing this erroneous line of reasoning, these people go as far as to suggest that such arrangements foster corruption, as people in my government prioritize personal gains over public welfare.

Obviously, these critics of my governing style fail to accept how important it is to be surrounded by loyal people. It is a *sine qua non* for any effective leadership. Like any other situation in life, loyalty overrules all else. After all, you can't do everything alone. I am understandably hesitant therefore to punish persons who are accused of corrupt activities. I'm sure that they're just trying to be helpful to me. In fact, whatever they're doing, I'm sure it is for the benefit of my form of governance. And it's important to understand that if I protect them, they will be indebted to me.

The same troublemakers insinuate that I am exploiting my position to maintain my grip on power—that I am out to amass wealth. They fail to see the obvious—that I need financial resources to reward my many loyal followers. Surely it is high time that more people appreciate the advantages of cronyism and nepotism. As I have said, I have to prioritize the interests of the people who support me over the welfare of the general population; how else am I to cement my hold on power? I maintain that to keep me in charge will benefit everybody.

A further complaint circulated by these resistant individuals regards the perceived misallocation of resources. They say that a lack of economic transparency hinders economic growth and development. Consequently—if they are to be believed—it will contribute to widespread poverty and inequality. To be quite frank, this drivel makes me laugh. How misguided people can be! Admittedly, running a successful dictatorship means being less worried about the welfare or the property rights of the ordinary citizen. It is your true supporters who count. And wouldn't you do the same in my position? What's so bad about taking care of the people who help you to stay in power? What difference does the odd dose of corruption make in the grand scheme of things?

Viktor Yanukovych, the former president of Ukraine, has been targeted as one of the examples of dictators who encouraged corrupt practices. If anybody suffered the wrath of bad press it was him. Why did people get so excited when they discovered—after he left the country—that he was the owner of an opulent mansion with a private exotic zoo? I know from personal experience that to be a dictator takes effort and vigilance; shouldn't such effort be rewarded? Unfortunately, Yanukovych is now living in exile in Russia with a miserly fortune of $100 million. People can be so unfair!

I am very much of a realist and acknowledge that there is corruption in any political system, democratic or otherwise. No political system can be perfect. I strongly believe that a dictatorship can be extremely effective in deterring all kinds of harmful behavior, and considering all its positives, corruption is not a big deal. Just look at Afghanistan. What previous governments weren't able to accomplish, its theocratic dictatorship is now getting it done. The country is safe. And I think that what is happening to their Shiite population is highly exaggerated. Even conceding that, there are far less explosions at their social gatherings, and let us not overlook how successful the Taliban has been in eliminating the drug trade. Therefore, in light of their success, why do we always need to make such a big stink about women's rights? And why make all this noise about the closure of hairdressing salons? Aren't there much better things to talk about? Also, why make their educational practices, or better, the lack of them, such a big deal?

If further examples were needed, look at all the good things Mohammed Bin Salman (MBS), the ruler of Saudi Arabia, has been doing for his country. Wasn't it a master stroke the way he took care of all these corrupt people, locking them up in Riyadh's Ritz-Carlton Hotel? And after some modest persuasion, I believe they coughed up about $100 billion. Given all the good he is doing for his country, to suggest that he should take some blame for the murder of this pesty journalist Khashoggi seems blatantly unfair. Now some people are also muttering about him having acquired a $450 million painting or a $300 million castle in France. This, I'm sure, is pure envy.

"HARD BUT NECESSARY"

I strongly believe that all my actions are motivated by noble ideals. In pursuit of these, I have had to make choices that can be called "hard but necessary" for the good of the nation. I cannot agree therefore with the Nobel Prize winner Albert Camus, who said, "The welfare of the people in particular has always been the alibi of tyrants." People don't realize that I am an idealist, that I am acting in the name of the people. And I'm sure that all of my colleagues think the same way.

I am convinced that President Bashar al-Assad of Syria thinks very much along the same line. It was only unfortunate that he was up against so many malcontents. But you have to give him real credit for his stamina when he managed to rise again. The same observation can be made about the dictator of Venezuela, Nicolás Maduro. I admire his tenacity in the face of people unable or unwilling to appreciate all the good he has done for his country. People who argue that he has violated the human rights of its citizens, plundered the country's natural resources, and driven a once prosperous nation into economic ruin due to his authoritarian rule are simply wrong. He is an idealist and a true role model.

CULTIVATING A PERSONALITY CULT

Stalin of Russia, Mao of China, Adolph Hitler of Germany, and Kim Il Sung of North Korea made human idols of themselves because they believed ardently in an ideal and strove to achieve it. All believed in the ultimate goodness of themselves and the unchallengeable rightness of their decisions. Clearly, there must have been good reason why they believed there to be no higher power and therefore no higher law than themselves. In fact, I have always admired the remarkable clarity with which they presented themselves and their skill at managing their self-image.

Their greatest critics, however, believe such personality cults to be the tradition of the worst authoritarian regimes. They argue that it distorts historical facts and, moreover, that it doesn't bode well for future dictatorships. But how wrong they can be! Just think about some of my most prominent predecessors. For example, dictator François Duvalier of Haiti fostered a personality cult that claimed he was the physical embodiment of the nation. This was a masterful way of keeping his troubled country together. Look now at how it is faring without him—it has degenerated into a mess and is rife with gang wars.

Next, look at Juan Perón, elected three times as president of Argentina. Everybody would love him and his wife Eva. Again, see the state of his country now in the hands of his incapable successors. The country's financial bankruptcy can hardly be blamed on him. Another great loss is that of the long-time ruler of Albania, Enver Hoxha. He put into place such a nice cult of personality, and now, following his death, everybody seems to want to leave the country. Surely, it again proves how important he was in keeping the country together. In fact, he seems to have been a real genius, a person who knew everything about everything.

Like Hoxha, I think it is admirable to be portrayed as a genius, a person able to make insightful remarks on virtually all facets of life, from culture to economics to military matters. Even better is to have statues of yourself erected everywhere. In fact, a dictator who truly recognized the importance of doing exactly that was Saparmurat Niyazov, the president of Turkmenistan from 1985 to 2006. How fantastic it must be to have a 12-meter-tall gold-plated statue of yourself in the capital, rotating so as to always face the sun. How wise, too, to share your knowledge and require all schools to use your ghostwritten book, the *Ruhnama*, as the primary text. It must have been a fantastic learning experience.

Speaking again of personality cults, I should not fail to mention Hun Sen, the prime minister of Cambodia, another person who knows the importance of this activity across his 38 years of power. As can be seen by everyone, he is another person who is doing God's work. Most recently, like so many times before, the populace has re-elected him as their leader, giving him again a landslide victory. Of course, as an enlightened leader he had made sure that nobody could or dared to challenge him. Presently, he seems to be also following the great example of the North Korean Kim dynasty by announcing that his son Hun Manet is going to succeed him. You have to give it to him that he is really a leader with remarkable foresight. Given his remarkable foresight, he seems to have said that the time has come to sacrifice and relinquish power to make way for a younger generation of leaders. But fortunately for everyone, to have the nation continue to benefit from his wisdom, he will continue as the head of the ruling party.

The leader of Rwanda, Paul Kagame, is also a great believer in continuity. As a true master in media management, his rule has now reached a 30-year milestone. That he has been accused of operating a murderous network, assassinating exiled opponents, can only be a blatant lie. Instead, he should be praised, not only for having brought an end to the atrocities that took place in his country, but also for the economic miracle that he has created. In fact, to the whole of Africa, Kagame should be the example of how a country needs to be run.

SOME EGGS MUST BE BROKEN

Of course, any dictator committed to doing God's work will leave a few casualties in their wake. But as the saying goes, you cannot make an omelet without breaking eggs. The only way to deal with malcontents and the great equalizer is a good dose of terror. It does help to have people toe the line. Clearly, Stalin knew what he was talking about when he said, "The death of one man is a tragedy. The death of millions is a statistic." If some people disagreed with him, it must have been because they were in some way defective, insane, malignant, or mercenary. And if tens of millions of people died due to his actions, it must have been for a good cause.

People intrinsically long for someone to take care of them, to protect them, to help them to make decisions. And I am making an incredible effort to protect my people from both internal and external dangers. Such dangers—be they real or imagined—have truly helped my cause. In fact, a good look at history shows how people like me arise and flourish during times of severe economic trouble: times when people are at their most anxious, distraught even at their uncertain future prospects. For once people are correct when they say that dictatorships do not grow out of strong and successful governments but out of weak and helpless ones. In fact, people who are hungry and unemployed seem to be the stuff of which successful dictatorships are made of.

Given all the good things I have been doing for the nation—how I have put it back on its feet after a period of great confusion—I truly wish that the people were more appreciative of my work. But despite all my efforts, many of my subjects *still* don't realize that the things that I am doing are in their best interest. Instead of all this democratic mumbo jumbo, I get things done; the country is much better organized. To achieve this, some ethical considerations need to be taken more loosely. I have never bought into the statement of Andrei Sakharov, the troublesome Soviet scientist and Nobel Prize winner, when he noted (referring to well-functioning societies):

> Intellectual freedom is essential—freedom to obtain and distribute information, freedom for open-minded and unfearing debate and freedom from pressure by officialdom and prejudices. Such freedom of thought is the only guarantee against an infection of people by mass myths, which, in the hands of treacherous hypocrites and demagogues, can be transformed into bloody dictatorship.

Being an intellectual himself, he should have really known better.

IN PRAISE OF THE UNEDUCATED

What many critics of my more autocratic form of government fail to appreciate is how much effort it takes to be a dictator. I recall the creativity required to enact dictator-friendly laws, overcome protests, and suppress the hooligans; and inevitably, there may have been some bloodshed. The stubbornness of some people can be tragic, especially those who fail to accept what's good for them. In my opinion, this is especially true for the well-educated. Ignorance really can be such a bliss. In fact, like has been said by another terrific role model, Donald Trump, I love ignorant people. But it can be hard work maintaining their ignorance.

There is one thing no dictator needs, and that's a well-educated middle class. These people can cause real trouble, which is why when I came to power, I went to such great lengths to manage the country's information flow. In particular, it was instantly clear to me that I needed to control the media. I needed to filter the spread of irritating knowledge. Fortunately, getting a grip on the media—restricting access to information and stifling independent journalism—has helped me not only to orchestrate public opinion but also to control critical thinking. Fortunately, I'm not alone in this realization; the famous figure of the French Revolution Maximilien Robespierre once said, "The secret of freedom lies in educating people, whereas the secret of tyranny is in keeping them ignorant." People may need enlightenment, but it needs to be my kind of enlightenment.

The idea of free speech is highly overrated anyway. Here, don't take me wrong; I do believe in freedom, but freedom for what? Freedom to do what I think is in the best interest of the country. In this context, I find the comment by the late US president Herbert Hoover makes a lot of sense: "It is a paradox that every dictator has climbed to power on the ladder of free speech. Immediately on attaining power each dictator has suppressed all free speech except his own."

Of course, I realize that the steps that I have taken to assure that people speak with one voice can lead to political instability and internal conflict. Some people have warned that the repression and exclusion of dissenting voices may fuel opposition movements, radicalization, protests, and even uprisings. Fortunately, I have learned how to take care of these matters, and in the course of doing so, I have become quite digitally savvy. For example, I have learned how effective face recognition surveyance technologies are and pride myself on the number of social media intervention techniques on hand to keep people in line.

As I have discovered, governing will be much more effective if you have a culture of silence and a complacent population. A lack of transparency is also important. Whatever I do, I think that it's best kept shielded from scrutiny. That's a key principle in every effective dictatorship. Some troublemakers accuse me of limiting independent journalism to this end. They say that I hamper critical thinking—that I don't allow for the free expression of opinions. They also suggest that I hinder the spread of knowledge, insinuating that I am inhibiting social progress. They even go as far as to accuse me of rewriting history, when I am in fact harmlessly tinkering with our present educational systems. I vehemently believe it is my right to do so, having discovered the biased nature of so many educational textbooks. No wonder that I have called for historical rewrites.

DRAWBACKS OF THE DIGITAL AGE

Some people have told me that despotism can only flourish in darkness. Unfortunately, in the digital world that we are living in, there seems to be too much light. We're victims of an information explosion. There is far too much information going around. Therefore, even though some people claim that our digital age facilitates dictatorships, I don't think that's completely true. Many people seem to see right through all the factoids that I am trying to propagate. Therefore, even though I accept the comments about the ease of spreading false information, given the information revolution, it has become much harder to run an effective dictatorship and maintain the illusion that I am the freely elected leader of the nation. And even though I have tried to muscle the press—locking up many journalists—people always seem to find other ways to spread lies about me. It is not easy to have them keep their mouth shut. It really bothers me that too many of my citizens continue to receive all this nonsensical information.

What has become clear to me is that the overly well-educated started to question what I am trying to feed them. In comparison, ignorant minds would serve me far better. I'm convinced that if that were the case, people would be more united in their opinions. Diversity of opinion only creates more objectified knowledge—a very threatening thought. At times, however, as a dictator, I have this dream whereby all the people who resist my rule would have a common neck so that I might be able to cut it off at once. In fact, if this dream could only be actualized, it would make my life much easier. Instead, what I'm forced to do is to educate the people such that there is only one common mind to delude.

FIGHT FACTS WITH FEAR

What has been called the "objective truth" has always been my greatest enemy. Fortunately, I have a highly effective psychological weapon at my disposal: fear. Making people fearful has turned out to be a great control mechanism. By frightening the populace, most people will see the advantage of sacrificing their basic freedoms and rule-of-law protections. If such an intervention doesn't work, there is always the option of locking up disloyal members of the population, or further still, making them disappear. My collaboration with the police (secret and otherwise) and the military has therefore always been of the utmost importance. And if locking up people doesn't make them more compliant, the time may come to make them disappear. In fact, often I have found that these disappearances can be highly effective. Not only is it the way to silence these malcontents, but it can also be a way of silencing their families and, by extension, society at large. In that respect, we can learn much from China's dictator, Xi Jinping. He has been a master in this particular intervention technique; I can only marvel at how he manages to frighten people in this incredibly large country. It seems the only way to go in suppressing certain opinions. Following his example, arbitrary arrests, detentions, torture, and even extrajudicial killings have turned out to be highly effective. Of course, poisoning people or having them fall from high places, like is such a laudable practice in Russia, also will put the fear of God into them.

PEOPLE MUST EXPECT THE UNEXPECTED

Like it or not, dictators often have no choice but to deal with dissent in a forceful manner. Understandably, as mentioned before, my sights have been trained on my natural enemies, namely political activists, journalists, and writers. It seems that strength and the threat of force are the only language these people seem to understand. Even I, however, acknowledge that the actions of some leaders can be excessive. The military leader of Myanmar, Min Aung Hlaing for example, may have gone too far; bombing your own people out of existence can give dictatorships a bad reputation. What I do appreciate, however, is his resoluteness. In his indifference to pleas from the UN and the international community and unwillingness to make a single concession, he demonstrates that he is a person of unwavering principles. Min Aung Hlaing has been just as skilled in another despotic tactic—unpredictability. Nothing is better at keeping the people on their toes than the uncertainty of whether they have followed the rules correctly.

What people fail to see is dealing with malcontents can be hard work. Sometimes it is like I am on a treadmill, suppressing one dissenter only to hear of another elsewhere, some being repeat offenders. Sometimes, it is difficult convincing even my soft-hearted supporters that these malingerers must be dealt with, not as human beings but as the hooligans they are, seemingly intent on destroying all the good work that I have been doing for my country. I am just fortunate that, like many other enlightened dictatorial leaders, I have become quite effective in inciting most of my supporters against them.

THE CLOAK AND DAGGER OF BELIEF

What has helped me in making my way of looking at things really stick is to wrap myself in the cloak of patriotism and religion. In fact, in getting my way, I have learned that it is highly commendable to exhibit an uncommon religious devotion. It seems the populace is far less apprehensive of what they may interpret as dramatic interventions if they believe that I am god-fearing and pious. Again, in this matter, Vladimir Putin has been my major role model. You can see how well he collaborates with the head of the Orthodox Church, Patriarch Kirill of Moscow. What a great duo they make.

In fact, Putin, as an ex-KGB colonel, really understands what is required of a dictator. Pretending that you are God's representative on earth can be seen as the prescription for preventing discontent. Of course, the last thing he wants to see is an event like the Orange Revolution in Ukraine. It has been a terrible example of how people, when not properly controlled, can put an end to a refined dictatorship. Putin knows, too, that when things go wrong, it doesn't necessarily make for a comfortable retirement situation.

Furthermore, what's also alleged is that dictatorships can lead to political instability and internal conflict. Critics who are unable to recognize the advantages of a dictatorship argue that the repression and exclusion of dissenting voices fuel opposition movements and make for radicalization. According to them, this will only incite protests, uprisings, or even civil war. Some of these malcontents have even suggested that dictators *start* wars, using the threat of external enemies to exert internal control over their own people. One of the former US presidents, James Madison said that "If tyranny and oppression comes to the land, it will be in the guise of fighting a foreign enemy." He believed that a lack of peaceful mechanisms to address grievances could escalate tensions and would endanger social cohesion. I have been asking myself if there is some truth in what he had said.

"BREAD AND CIRCUSES"

It may be worthwhile to mention that a palliative offering can act to avert potential discontent. I have made a great effort to give the people "bread and circuses," to use this well-known Roman expression. As a dictator, I have always known that you have to keep people's stomachs full and their heads empty. They will come to realize that they cannot eat the freedom that supposedly comes with democracy.

But in case of potential unrest—when I am unable to provide these bread and games—I have to do other things to divert people's minds from the concerns they may have about me. Another weapon I therefore keep in my arsenal is to call on scapegoats. After all, the easiest hunt in the world will always be the hunt for scapegoats. It is especially handy to use minority groups as people who can be blamed for a nation's troubles. I have become skilled at inciting hatred against ethnic, religious, and other minority groups. This has always been a foolproof way to solidify my dictatorial powers.

Patriotism remains one of the greatest ways to maintain your powerbase. Plato was right that "When the tyrant has disposed of foreign enemies by conquest . . . and there is nothing to fear from them, then he is always stirring up some war." I wonder whether this was the reason why Putin started his "special military operation." As a very thoughtful, rational individual, I'm sure that he is going to be successful. People who argue that this war will turn out to be the strategic mistake of the century should be called what they are: spoilsports. However, as I have watched this war proceed, I start wondering whether these pessimists may have a point. Is Putin really behaving, as some people have suggested, like a cornered rat?

Unfortunately, there seem to be many complainers who accuse Putin of living in a bubble. They say that he has been distancing himself too much. They point out petty details like his seating arrangements at conferences, but I merely think he is being prudently cautious—you never know what germs other people are harboring. Still, there are some people who think that he is only receiving filtered information. But what could also be true is that his key lieutenants carry out his orders before they are given, perhaps even before he has thought of these orders. It could very well be that his key lieutenants are going much further in making decisions for him than he would ideally like. It makes me wonder whether the same is true for the people I'm dealing with.

THE INVERSION OF FEAR

At times, I ask myself whether people realize the amount of stress I live under. Truth be told, the life of a dictator is not for sissies. The Greek playwright Aeschylus once said that "In every tyrant's heart there springs in the end this poison, that he cannot trust a friend." Perhaps there is some truth in his words. I have grown increasingly mistrustful of the people I'm dealing with; I am no longer sure who I can rely on. I imagine that there is always the chance that some kind of "crazy" individual will try to kill me. If I am honest, this thought is haunting me every moment of the day and night. Isn't it sad that as a dictator, you can never feel really safe? I find myself wondering how well Aleksandr Lukashenko of Belarus sleeps at night with such a thankless population outside. Fortunately, he has the eternal friendship of Putin, like Putin has the eternal friendship of Xi Jinping of China.

Lukanshenko's example illustrates once more that dictators, despite all their good intentions, do not always have the love of their people. Some such dictators may even fear their people. It makes me wonder how well my compatriots in America and Africa sleep at night. In particular, I'm thinking of José Daniel Ortega Saavedra of Nicaragua, Nicolás Maduro of Venezuela, or my colleague dictator Emmerson Mnangagwa of Zimbabwe. Frankly speaking, my heart goes out to all of them. We need to do more to support each other. These leaders are such obvious examples of people who seem to be misunderstood. While they're making great efforts to take care of their citizens, it is unbelievable that so many people don't realize what is in their best interests. Sadly enough, it seems that the philosopher George Santayana had a point when he said, "Tyrants are seldom free; the cares and the instruments of their tyranny enslave them." Like my fantasy about the populace, a dictator has but one throat to slit.

When I need to boost my morale, I bring to mind a notion courtesy of the French philosopher Voltaire that "Clever tyrants are never punished." Unfortunately, Winston Churchill's statement is similarly memorable when he said, "Dictators ride to and fro upon tigers which they dare not dismount. And the tigers are getting hungry." Whether that's the case in my country, I am not so sure. However, if I am truly honest with myself, my nightmare scenario is what has happened to Nicolae Ceauşescu, Saddam Hussein, and Muammar Gadhafi. To kill them! People can be so cruel! Tragically enough, it appears that dictatorships are never as strong as they imagine them to be. And people are never as weak as they think they are. The last thing I would want is for people to discover that I am actually a very frightened man.

Once, I read that a dictatorship can be compared to a magnificent tree that was impressive to look at but seemed to lack roots. It didn't take very much for it to fall. According to the Argentinian writer Jorge Luis Borges, "Dictatorships foster oppression, dictatorships foster servitude, dictatorships foster cruelty; more abominable is the fact that they foster idiocy." If he wasn't already dead, I would have locked him up. The crazy things people dare to say! Freedom of speech is definitely overrated.

8

THE RISE OF THE LEVIATHAN

In that day the Lord with his sore and great and strong sword shall punish leviathan the piercing serpent, even leviathan that crooked serpent; and he shall slay the dragon that is in the sea.

—Isaiah 27:1

LEVIATHAN called a COMMONWEALTH, or STATE (in Latin, CIVITAS), which is but an artificial man, though of greater stature and strength than the natural, for whose protection and defense it was intended; and in which the sovereignty is an artificial soul, as giving life and motion to the whole body.

—Thomas Hobbes

THIS TERRIFYING SERPENT

After the satirical approach of the previous chapter, it is now necessary to have a more sober and in-depth discussion regarding the dynamics of these people's leadership style. In previous chapters, I have already described some of the personality traits associated

DOI: 10.4324/9781003427117-9

with demagogue-like populist leaders. Now, I adopt a more reflective position to examine the cunning means by which these people rise to positions of power. It strikes me that the English political philosopher Thomas Hobbes can help shed some light on this. Hobbes is best known for his 1651 book *Leviathan*, in which he expounds on the importance of social contract theory and demonstrates the need for a strong central authority to prevent the evil of discord and civil war. According to Hobbes, effective government requires absolute authority, and the only way to avoid war is through a strong, unified government ruled by an absolute sovereign, the Leviathan.

In Jewish mythology, the Leviathan is a primordial sea serpent, a monstrous creature symbolizing evil and challenging God. According to the scriptures, it needs to be slain by God in order for the world to be restored to its natural balance. Over time, however, the Leviathan has come to have many other symbolic meanings. It has come to represent God's power of creation, a beast of Satan, or a dark force; it has been an avatar for chaos and anarchy, an embodiment of the abuse of power, and an expression of willful ignorance. Perhaps most fundamental to all of these, it is a symbol of authoritarianism.

For Hobbes, this latter interpretation was true—he saw the Leviathan as a metaphor for the ideal state—a commonwealth in which all people would be united under a single sovereign power. Interestingly, the frontispiece of the first edition of Hobbes' *Leviathan*, which he helped design, portrays the commonwealth as a gigantic human figure built out of the bodies of its citizens, with the sovereign as its head. Hobbes examined the relationship between society and its rulers in his political treatise. He posited that human beings have a natural inclination to war and suggested that the world needs a Leviathan to preserve the peace.

Hobbes proclaimed that only an absolute ruler, the Leviathan, wielding near-unlimited power, is able to maintain order over the chaotic, selfish, and sinful masses. Thus, he advocated for a social contract in which those governed accept the absolute power of the sovereign in exchange for a guarantee of peace and security. It is evident from these propositions that Hobbes, like the dictator in the previous chapter, wasn't an advocate of democratic governance. While he put forth these ideas in an attempt to prevent discord and civil war, they bear a striking resemblance to a blueprint for creating a police state. Ironically, whether Hobbes realized it or not, Biblical texts always depicted the Leviathan as an object of evil—an entity through which Satan wages war against God and His people.

THREATS TO CIVIL SOCIETY

As the previous chapters have stressed, the world is full of Leviathans. Democracies and democratic institutions are very fragile entities. Countries as diverse as China, Russia, Belarus, Turkey, Hungary, the Philippines, Brazil, Venezuela, Rwanda, Egypt, India, Israel, or Saudi Arabia exemplify the grave threats facing civil society. In many countries, we observe questionable electoral practices, a lack of independence in judiciary appointments, extensive media manipulation, pervasive corruption and cronyism, and systemic attempts to suppress dissent. Even in so-called established democracies like the United States, the United Kingdom, or Israel, the threat of rule by a Leviathan remains an ever-present and realistic prospect.

It appears presently that democracy is experiencing something of a mid-life crisis. The mere fact that a flawed individual like Donald Trump could have been elected as president of the United States exemplifies this clear and present danger. Various political observers, mainly from China, have been suggesting that Western democracies have outlived their usefulness and are showing many signs of decay. Others, as discussed in Chapters 5 and 6, attribute the demise of democracy to the ascent of populism. These critics contend that the leaders advocating democratic governance have failed to empower their citizens. The people find themselves lagging behind economically, unable to lead dignified lives, and blaming their situation on their governments. It is clear that without economic prosperity for all, it is a challenge for democracies to thrive. When people are fearful of what the future will bring, they often look for miracle workers who promise instant solutions. Unfortunately, in many instances, these miracle workers will favor more Leviathan forms of government.

THE RISE OF THE NEO-AUTOCRATS

When you hear the words "despot," "tyrant," "dictator," or "autocrat," what comes to mind? Do you imagine an ill-tempered king sitting on a throne, screaming orders for the execution of those who dare disobey him? Do figures such as Idi Amin, Adolph Hitler, Joseph Stalin, Ivan the Terrible, Attila the Hun, Vlad the Impaler, or Genghis Khan come to mind? Considering the toxic nature of these leaders, one cannot help but ask the question: What is it about Leviathan-style leadership practices that appeals to people? Why do leaders and their followers continue to embrace autocratic forms of governance?

The Cult of Personality

History has shown time and time again that certain personality types are more likely to rise to positions of power. Leviathan leaders, these autocratic types, possess strikingly similar characteristics to populist leaders. Many are considered charismatic, yet behind their charismatic veneer lies a very calculating personality. They tend to be a combination of the narcissistic and antisocial (psychopathic) personality type, possessing qualities such as a lack of empathy, feelings of grandiosity, a thirst for power and control, feelings of entitlement, a sense of vindictiveness, a Machiavellian nature, and an indifference to conventional laws, rules, or morality. Such people can be labeled "malignant narcissists."

Of course, these leaders do not and cannot rise in a vacuum. This raises the critical question: What is it about human nature that attracts people to these autocratic rulers? Why are people so easily bamboozled and willing to have these individuals control their lives? Do they not recognize the dark forces that these Leviathans represent?

In previous chapters, I have pointed out how easily humans regress under stress and display dependency reactions, looking for strong leaders to provide guidance. In addition to capitalizing on these regressive behavioral patterns, autocrats have found additional methods to deceive and manipulate the people who idolize them.

To prevent their subjects from realizing their true nature, leaders who advocate Leviathan-style governance find ways to maintain a more acceptable facade. (The installment plan scenario to power as discussed in the previous chapter seems to be one way to make it happen.) Rather than embodying the ferocity associated with the Leviathan, a creature emblematic of tyranny, they devise subtler methods to subjugate and subdue their people. Unlike historical dictators such as Hitler, Stalin, or Mao, many of the contemporary Leviathan rulers do not exhibit overtly draconian behavior. Instead of using excessive violence, they would employ force in a more subtle and disguised way. Deception and seduction are prioritized as means of securing the voluntary obedience of their subjects. In this regard, they can be described as "neo-autocrats."

Although they sometimes profess allegiance to democratic politics, in reality, these neo-autocrats use complicated and contradictory webs of regulations to maintain their powerbase and police every area of their subjects' lives. Essentially, they create a phantom democracy. What makes their behavior even more sinister is their ability to present directives as exercises of freedom and choice. For example, the act of voting in elections and referendums, which seemingly offers people the freedom of choice, is in reality predetermined within the convoluted political framework they have created. These neo-autocrats are very talented at crafting the "illusion of choice."

These neo-autocrats manipulate the law, selectively employing it to target their opponents while finding legal loopholes to shield themselves and their cliques from any threats to their power. In other words, they excel at exploiting the rule of law to undermine the rule of law. When they assume control of the judiciary, they have the ability to shape and control the laws to suit their interests. Their unpredictable tactics instill docility and fear among their subjects, leading them to behave like domesticated animals, like these sheeples. The Leviathan will not devour its subjects as long as they toe the line, do what the state requires, and don't cause any trouble. It is evident that these neo-autocrats have amalgamated centralized power with pseudo-democratic processes. And this kind of society created by neo-autocratic leaders is so effectively portrayed in the scene that was described in Chapter 4 from Sacha Baron Cohen's film, *The Dictator*.

Undoubtedly, Sacha Baron Cohen portrayed a form of autocratic leadership that cleverly masked itself behind an appealing facade. Again, it demonstrates behavior that involves skillfully blending centralized power with democratic processes. Outwardly, these leaders affirm their allegiance to the rules of civil society, while in reality their neo-autocratic approach is disguised as a pseudo-democracy. These leaders excel at manipulating the lives of their constituents, marshaling their support, and enforcing conformity. The underlying essence of their rule is organized lawlessness, which explains why they pay lip service to democratic processes, pretend to support elections, and supposedly launch anti-corruption campaigns. In essence, they seduce their subjects by mimicking democratic structures while effectively exploiting the governance procedures of society for their own benefit.

Neo-autocratic leadership can exhibit a range of characteristics, varying from relatively benign to extremely despotic. For example, again take Rwandan President Paul Kagame. While many Rwandans seem to revere their president for the progress their country made during his many years in office, others are criticizing him for suppressing dissenting views. Following the genocide against the Tutsi community, Kagame's Rwandan Patriotic Front determined that the country should transition towards what has been euphemistically referred to as a "consensual democracy," a form of governance with the goal of preventing further ethnic violence. Although this model brought stability and facilitated a remarkable economic recovery, it eventually evolved into a pseudo-democratic system where few individuals would dare challenge Kagame's authority. Essentially, it demonstrates that when an autocrat can ensure wealth and stability, people may be more inclined to overlook their loss of liberty. If these neo-autocrats are perceived as delivering on economic goals, the democratic shortcomings of their leadership tend to be easily excused.

But is it truly worth the risk to accept such a form of governance? Could it be the start of a perilous descent into the abyss? After all, it is widely acknowledged that philosopher-kings have always been a rarity. All too often, these neo-autocrats tend to slide down the slippery slope of power abuse, with extreme cases like North Korea, Eritrea, Venezuela, or Myanmar serving as stark examples. However, despite the risks associated with the creation of these Leviathan-style governments, many people still find these neo-autocrats alluring. This begs the question: What is the secret behind these leaders' charm?

The prevailing factor that contributes to the appeal of Leviathan governance is the reality of living in an age of anxiety. There is much to be scared about, and people fear that things will fall apart. It is this state of mind that makes neo-authoritarianism so attractive, particularly when the alternative appears to be chaos. Hence, as has been said repetitively, individuals tend to regress into a state of dependency and hope that the Leviathan will save them. This may help explain the lingering nostalgia for rulers like Stalin and Mao, who, despite their atrocities, provided their people with a semblance of social order.

The Search for Parental Protection

As has been pointed out before, in a state of dependency, humans gravitate towards some form of higher authority or power that can offer them protection. Originally, parental figures were the ones individuals turned to for protection in times of threat. Consequently, when people are anxious, their need for the support of a strong, seemingly perfect, and powerful parental figure intensifies. Often, when people feel a lack of control over their lives, they turn to imagined figures or escapist outlets to regain a sense of power. Sometimes, they may even turn to religion and its representations of all-powerful idealized figures. However, more commonly, they seek solace in familiar people in their lives, whether they are celebrities, idols, or individuals who exude self-confidence. They seek charismatic figures who can save them.

Neo-autocratic leaders possess a keen understanding of how to exploit people who are plagued by anxiety. They take advantage of this deep-rooted need for a savior, someone who can provide a sense of security in a highly insecure world. As these neo-autocrats know how to present themselves with great outward confidence and self-assuredness, they become particularly attractive to those who feel unsteady or insecure in themselves.

GOING INTO THE ABYSS

Considering the conscious and unconscious psychological dynamics at play, what specific actions do these leaders take to rise to power? What do they do to make the idea of the Leviathan rule acceptable to the masses? Given what has been said in the previous chapters about living in a psychotic age, being a sheeple, feeling wronged, and the seductiveness of populism, what are the actions that these people take?

1) Regardless of their political leaning, neo-autocrats often present themselves as representatives of the common people. They tell people what they want to hear, even if their promises are totally illogical from a rational standpoint. One effective method they employ to rouse their audience is, as has been mentioned before, the cultivation of a sense of victimization. A sense of victimization, fueled by emotional contagion, can be an immensely powerful force, with anger and envy being particularly potent emotions. Subsequently, these neo-autocrats present themselves as defenders, claiming to shield their audiences from the arrogant elites and unworthy outsiders whom they refer to as enemies of the people. They implore their supporters to join them in the righteous fight against these adversaries.

2) In order to establish their powerbase and rally followers to join their fight, neo-autocrats must manipulate both hearts and minds. As mentioned before, these leaders excel in communication and utilize the media to control the dissemination of information. They embrace the abundance of communication

channels and exploit them to their advantage. They are masters at choreographing great public appearances, know how to plug potential avenues of criticism, and expertly orchestrate fake news. They hold a disdain for journalists, and, if they cannot buy their loyalty, they may try to persecute them.

3) As the previous chapter pointed out, these neo-autocrats are also adept at inventing ideologies, whether religious or otherwise. They recognize how important it is to create systems of ideas and ideals that cement their powerbase. In fact, throughout history, leaders have used existing religions or ideologies or, in certain instances, even fabricated new ones to introduce their Leviathan rule. These systems of ideas conveniently justify why the leader should occupy the role for life, and sometimes even why the post should pass to the leader's descendants. North Korea serves as an extreme example of this phenomenon.

4) Once in power, neo-autocrats shrewdly create the illusion of choice during elections. They strategically stage voting procedures in a way that leads voters to believe they can make a difference. However, the reality is that decisions have already been predetermined, rendering the voting process more like an optical illusion. In order to assure the desired outcome, they resort to draconian measures to prevent dissent and other points of view from emerging. Possible opponents may be disqualified or imprisoned.

5) After neutralizing opposition, neo-autocrats become dependent on the support of their trusted cronies and family members to assure their hold on power. They rely on kinship networks, loyalists, and factotums because life at the top can be full of risk and danger. They are astutely aware that power needs to be tightly regulated and carefully guarded. Furthermore (also mentioned in the previous chapter), these leaders realize that they cannot survive for long without cultivating alliances with the military and the police (secret or otherwise). Many of these neo-autocrats also have had military backgrounds, as exemplified by former dictator presidents such as Pervez Musharraf

of Pakistan, Mobutu Sese Seko of the Democratic Republic of the Congo, and Idi Amin of Uganda. All three were high-ranking army officers who co-opted the military to overthrow governments and implement more Leviathan governance structures. Present-day leaders like Paul Kagame of Rwanda or Abdel Fattah El-Sisi of Egypt share a similar background as former military officers.

6) Neo-autocrats also excel at carefully managing the emerging middle class. They realize the importance of keeping this group satisfied, as they tend to be a potential source of disquiet and dispute. This group is often considered prime candidates for rebellion as they are better educated and more aware of what's going on. To keep them in line, neo-autocrats exploit the fact that the middle class admires the unattainable riches of the elites while looking down upon the hardships faced by the poor. They leverage the power of status-based symbols and bribe this class by capitalizing on their position within the social hierarchy. Encouraging hedonism and hyper-consumerism, they entice the middle class with small material possessions or luxury experiences, such as vacations. These small rewards encourage the middle classes to support the Leviathan and turn a blind eye to any wrongdoing. For the broader population, neo-autocratic leaders offer trinkets in the form of government handouts, token welfare programs, dazzling televised gala events, and shiny construction projects.

7) Finally, in case of trouble or if the populace becomes restless, neo-autocrats can always point to external threats to justify their existence. In this regard, war and the presence of a common enemy serve as the ultimate diversionary tactic. To garner support, neo-autocrats must project themselves as defenders rather than warmongers. Again, Putin's "special military operation" is an apt example of this. If successful, they can seal their reputation as great leaders, much like legendary warlords such as Alexander the Great, Julius Caesar, Genghis Khan, or Napoleon, who are now regarded as military geniuses for expanding their nations' territories through invading their neighbors.

A THREAT TO WORLD STABILITY

It is important to recognize that Leviathan rule not only leads to economic and psychological deprivation for the people of a country, but its negative influence may extend beyond national borders. As we have seen repeatedly, neo-autocrats use both internal and external threats to pacify their subjects. Consequently, this form of governance threatens international peace. In the interconnected world of the 21st century, the problems of one nation can easily become those of its neighbors as well. The existence of neo-autocratic rulers ought to be a global concern, as demonstrated by the recent devastating war in Ukraine.

The danger posed by the Leviathan is ever-present, influenced by the evolutionary and psychodynamic processes that govern human behavior. And as has been indicated, apathy, indifference, and deprivation can stifle democratic processes. Similarly, to the "boiled frog syndrome," the populace may not realize that they are slowly being "cooked" until it is too late.

Indeed, humans have (and always will) struggled with the need to be led and the desire to be free. Reconciling these two forces will always prove difficult. The allure of Leviathan governance lies in the desire to be led, controlled, and have all problems resolved by an omnipotent power. Hence, as mentioned previously, counteracting forces are needed to resist the seductive nature of Leviathan, including strong civil institutions that provide checks and balances (such as an independent judiciary and an independent press) and a well-educated population that has embraced a civil mindset. Without these elements, a country will easily regress into Leviathan governance, with its population exhibiting zombie-like behavior.

It has also become quite clear that Leviathan governance doesn't pave the way for a progressive, vibrant society or contribute to economic and sociocultural development. On the contrary, despite all its hiccups and messiness, a well-run democracy allows people to live a life of prosperity and happiness. Unfortunately, understanding these necessary conditions doesn't guarantee that things will turn out this way. Writer and philosopher Aldous Huxley succinctly captured this notion when he wrote, "So long as men worship the Caesars and Napoleons, Caesars and Napoleons will duly arise and make them miserable."

Hanging on to a Leviathan can easily lead a country into war, a subject that will be discussed in more detail in the next chapter. Ernest Hemingway, who witnessed war at close quarters, offered a profound observation: "Never think that war, no matter how necessary, nor how justified, is not a crime." Indeed, we should ponder the consequences if we fail to bring an end to war. What will happen to the human race? Can even the survivors truly survive the ravages of war?

9

THE HORRORS OF WAR

A great war leaves the country with three armies: an army of cripples, an army of mourners, and an army of thieves.

—German proverb

The supreme art of war is to subdue the enemy without fighting.

—Sun Tzu

THE FOG OF WAR

War—what a glorious adventure! How exciting it will be! What better way to enact heroic deeds that showcase the finest of human qualities—idealism, courage, and self-sacrifice? What thrills! What fun, courage, and self-sacrifice! And what a great way to find purpose, meaning, and a reason for living!

War makes life deceptively simple. It capitalizes on the black-and-white thinking articulated in earlier chapters and establishes clear distinctions between right and wrong, good and bad, saints and sinners, and winners and losers.

DOI: 10.4324/9781003427117-10

But are wars truly heroic? Do they really bring out the best in people? Referring to wars as "glorious" may even appear as a psychopathic tendency. In reality, wars are barbaric, and their only certainty is death and devastation. They don't have great endings, seldom resolve problems, and are an entirely destructive response to conflicts. There are far better approaches, as highlighted by American novelist Margaret Atwood when she stated, "War is what happens when language fails." War is an exercise in brutality, futility, and stupidity, the more recent ones in Ukraine and Gaza terrifying examples.

Conflicts often begin because leaders fail to realize that fighting causes more problems than it resolves. Even the act of celebrating a victory is questionable. Far too frequently, nations that win wars suffer the loss of peace. In reality, there is truly no way to emerge as a winner. I strongly believe that nothing that war has ever achieved couldn't have been achieved without it.

Wars will always be an abomination. They destroy the very foundations of humanity and lead to despicable deeds that cannot be captured in words alone. In war, acts of rape and plunder become distressingly commonplace, and the line between right and wrong can become blurred. As the philosopher Bertrand Russell pointedly said, "War does not determine who is right—only who is left." The tragedy of war is that it exploits the best in people to commit the most abhorrent actions. On this point German statesman Otto von Bismarck wisely cautioned, "Anyone who has ever looked into the glazed eyes of a soldier dying on the battlefield will think hard before starting a war." The war between Russia and Ukraine clearly demonstrates the unspeakable horrors that accompany war. The avalanche of war crimes occurring in Ukraine demonstrates how this war has encouraged human regression. Such battles do not bring out the best in people; they unleash the beasts in them. And what has been happening in Sudan, the Democratic Republic of the Congo, Ukraine, and Gaza show once more how man can be a wolf to another man.

Due to the atrocities, the healing process in the aftermath of war will be a different, difficult kind of battle itself; the struggle can linger for centuries and even beyond. There is nothing glamorous or romantic about it; war is the only game in which both parties lose As aptly expressed by French writer Antoine de Saint-Exupery, "War is not an adventure. It is a disease. It is like typhus." Surviving may be the only glory.

TURNING A BLIND EYE

Despite the harrowing reality of war, many seem willing to ignore its true nature. They prefer to remain oblivious to the fact that death and emotional devastation are inherent to any armed conflict. Many of the people volunteering for battle share an illusion of immortality, confident that they will be one of the survivors, emerging unscathed while others are injured or killed. They forget that, in war, there are no unwounded soldiers. Even if they return physically unscathed, no soldier escapes the psychological repercussions of war. As Benjamin Franklin noted, "Wars are not paid for in wartime, the bill comes later." Wars disturb the natural order of life and turn man on man in the most inhuman way. To emphasize this point, the Greek historian Herodotus once said, "In peace, sons bury their fathers. In war, fathers bury their sons." Indeed, war will always be about the betrayal of the young by the old.

Any close examination of human history exposes the harsh reality of wars. Ever since notions of territory and ownership have existed, humans have been embroiled in conflicts. Violence and brute force have always been the preferred ways of settling issues. Wars have plagued thousands of countries across multiple millennia, resulting in countless lives lost.

THE SAVAGE BEAST

Considering the ubiquity of war, it appears that primal, savage instinct resides within every person. When armed, this instinct can manifest in truly devastating ways. American naturalist Henry David Thoreau highlighted this human characteristic by stating, "The savage in man is never quite eradicated." As a result, war has always been part of the so-called natural state of humankind.

Despite its horrors, many people attempt to rationalize war as a necessary evil. Some even suggest that war is the only and inevitable path to peace. Given the destruction it wreaks, we must question the nature and longevity of whatever peace it will bring. Still, even with a litany of wars behind us, the world remains as divided as it has ever been. Religious and ideological strife persists wherever we turn, and the lack of civic behavior—that bedrock of civil society—is missing.

War therefore is deeply ingrained in our nature and in times of conflict serves as our default mode of operation. To borrow the words of German philosopher Immanuel Kant, "With men, the state of nature is not a state of peace, but war." In light of this observation, we should ask ourselves whether war is an interlude during peace or is peace an interlude during war. Peace is often the short interval during which nations toil to pay the costs of past and future wars.

MOUNDS OF CORPSES

It is my belief that war has never accomplished anything that couldn't have been achieved through alternative means. In fact, wars do not provide lasting solutions; instead, they only create more problems for the future. Nor do they contribute to the creation of a better world. Building a civilization on mounds of corpses is not a means by which humanity should progress. There are always more effective ways to move forward.

The central question arises: What is needed to make leaders realize that the use of force is an extremely poor and regressive approach to problem-solving? The desire to start a war can be compared to the kneejerk reactions commonly observed among small children when they get angry. However, with children, there is the hope that as they develop into full-grown, mature human beings, they will find other ways of acting out or verbalizing their frustrations and become more introspective. Can we not expect the same from those in leadership positions? Should they not be able to reflect and recognize that taking a warlike position is not a progressive way forward?

Leaders need to realize that war grants people permission to commit barbaric acts and that the restraints and boundaries established by civilized society are eroded in its midst. Psychiatrist and Holocaust survivor Victor Frankl emphasized this truth: "Since Auschwitz we know what man is capable of. And since Hiroshima we know what is at stake." In times of war, humans are capable of doing the most horrendous things.

In essence, when an individual shoots another person, they are deemed a murderer; however, if a leader sends millions of people to their death, they may be hailed as heroic. The French philosopher Voltaire noted this human duplicity when he stated, "It is forbidden to kill; therefore, all murderers are punished unless they kill in large numbers and to the sound of trumpets." In fact, every act of violence committed during war would be considered a crime in times of peace. What's so absurd and monstrous about wars is that people who have no personal quarrel are compelled to murder one another in cold blood. In reality, war is nothing more than a grotesque exercise in serial killing.

As technology develops, our wars have become increasingly devastating in their reach. They no longer consist of a few people throwing rocks at one another, causing relatively little harm. When we contemplate the prospect of war in today's society, we should be concerned about the survival of our species as a whole. Humans have developed incredibly advanced technology, which amplifies the destructive potential of warfare. As things stand, it is clear that humans are edging closer to nuclear war and environmental catastrophe. As the English writer Herbert George Wells remarked, "If we don't end war, war will end us." Now, more than ever, no civilization can wage war without losing the right to be called civilized. To quote science fiction writer Isaac Asimov, "The mere existence of nuclear weapons by the thousands is an incontrovertible sign of human insanity." Starting a war these days is akin to inviting self-annihilation.

POWER CORRUPTS, ABSOLUTE POWER CORRUPTS ABSOLUTELY

Why then do leaders decide to initiate wars knowing full well the devastating implications? One way of understanding the question involves examining the mindset of people in positions of power. Being in a leadership position does not always foster optimal mental well-being, and there is always a delicate balance between personal disposition and the demands that position requires.

As I have explored throughout these chapters, certain personality types are more likely to seek out leadership positions. Attaining those positions carries significant psychological implications. Most likely, people aiming for power are no strangers to narcissism. However, when in power, the allure of narcissism is only stronger; leaders may end up living in an echo chamber, detached from the reality of everyday life, with subordinates inclined to tell them what they want to hear. Unfortunately, whilst in this narcissistic haze, they tend to be prone to illusions of grandiosity, whilst simultaneously experiencing anxiety and fear that their power may be taken away from them. Hence, delusions of persecution may also manifest. After all, paranoia is the malady of kings.[1] It doesn't take much, especially in the absence of civil safeguards, for such egotistical leaders to descend into autocracy or even despotism. Historically, neither state has ever proven to be the most effective way to rule a country.

As I have also pointed out in the previous chapters, one strategy often deployed by leaders attempting to consolidate their powerbase and maintain control over their populace is to create a common enemy and engage in war against them. Moreover, the likelihood of people desiring a change in government diminishes during times of war. The looming threat of conflict engenders an anxiety and tendency to develop a dependency position, clamoring for a leader to show the way. War is the ideal catalyst for fostering this kind of behavior. Sadly, people fail to realize the steep price they will pay for this temporary illusion of feeling protected.

THE THREE PS

Toxic leaders can be virtuosos in rallying the population to their cause. They are well acquainted with the three Ps of the demagogue-like leadership dynamics that I have previously touched upon: Populism, Polarization, and Propaganda. First, these leaders adopt populist tactics, creating imaginary realities that appeal to the needs and desires of their followers. They are highly effective snake oil salesmen. Second, they skillfully employ polarization, using primitive psychological defense mechanisms such as splitting and projection. In other words, they create a world of "us" (good) versus "them" (bad). Naturally, they are quick to place the blame on others when things go wrong. Third, they build a world based on alternative facts. As Greek philosopher Aeschylus once said, "In war, truth is the first casualty." The populace is offered conscience-soothing falsities while the truth is replaced by persuasive propaganda. Enforced by the military and the police, these rulers apply these three Ps of dysfunctional leadership as a means of instilling fear sufficient to guarantee their subjects' obedience. In the meantime, freedom of expression falls by the wayside.

These toxic leaders are masters at making their subjects believe they're fighting a righteous war and not, as they are, creating hell on earth. Faith in the righteousness of their cause overrides all reason, sense, and understanding. Whenever ideology or religion takes precedence, any sense of rationality is lost. Absolute truth transforms into blind truth, and anyone who questions the war is branded as a traitor. Those who fail to conform may end up imprisoned or silenced.

Leaders who live in these narcissistic bubbles and wage futile wars don't care that they're doing great harm to civil society. Not only do they sow seeds of mistrust and insecurity by spreading lies and encouraging hatred, but they also destroy generations and generations of values and culture. They make a mockery of human rights and, through their destructive actions, drive a whole nation insane.

THE NEED FOR REFLECTIVE LEADERS

Leaders who possess an inclination towards war are evidently not at peace with themselves. Their desire to fight should be seen as a symptom of a disturbed state of mind. Their inner world seems to be ruled by primitive emotions, lacking a substantial capacity for reflection. As American writer John Steinbeck noted, "All war is a symptom of man's failure as a thinking animal." The true battle they should be fighting is the one taking place in their minds. What they don't realize is that until they end the war in their mind, the real war will never end.

However, maintaining peace among humans will always be hard work. Therefore, various measures, both psychological and institutional, need to be taken in order to prevent demagogue-like leaders from coming to the fore in the first place and inciting unnecessary wars. What can't be emphasized enough is that a major countervailing force against toxic leadership will be the presence of an educated, psychologically savvy electorate. The voting public needs to be cognizant of the three Ps of dysfunctional leadership. Furthermore, strong civic institutional structures need to be in place to prevent such overt abuses of power.

It remains the ultimate challenge to tame the "beast" in all humankind when the call of war is so pervasive. Providentially, throughout history, it has been those who advocate peace, rather than those who promote war, who are revered. The people we admire most are the ones who preach non-violence and recognize that true victory lies in preventing war altogether. The slogan "make love, not war" is perhaps one of the most profound statements ever made. Compassion and empathy are essential qualities that bring out the best in human beings. Possessing the capacity to better relate and understand other people's experiences is the best way to avoid conflict.

What needs to be stressed is that only an early start in cultivating this compassion will prevent war-like attitudes from coming to the fore. In this regard, the words of Mahatma Gandhi are prophetic. He said, "If we are to teach real peace in this world, and if we are to carry on a real war against war, we shall have to begin with the children." In other words, in order to transcend humanity's inherent inclination towards war, we need to start early. Children should be exposed to the concept, specifics, nature, and ethical ambiguities of war from an early age to help them understand its horrors. Children must realize that while conflict is inevitable, going to war is not the way to solve issues.

If we succeed in making our children aware of the destructive nature of war, we can help them develop into reflective adults. This will allow them to develop qualities such as intimacy, generativity, and integrity, which are vital for responsible conflict resolution. In addition, possessing such qualities will contribute to responsible participation within institutions, a prerequisite for the creation and maintenance of strong civic institutions. In turn, the world will need leaders who subscribe to such a worldview. Thus, while effective leaders have a primary responsibility to prevent war, educators bear the primary task of ensuring peace.

NOTE

[1] Manfred F. R. Kets de Vries (2005). *Lessons on Leadership by Terror: Finding Shaka Zulu in the Attic*. London: Edward Elgar.

CONCLUDING COMMENTS

You cannot prevent the birds of sorrow from flying over your head, but you can prevent them from building nests in your hair.

—Chinese proverb

Nations which don't find their national identities will be preyed upon by other nations.

—Mustafa Kemal Ataturk

We may have different religions, different languages, different colored skin, but we all belong to one human race.

—Kofi Annan

A COUNTRY'S LEADERSHIP BRAND

Through the macro-psychological path that characterizes the chapters in this book, I have attempted to elucidate certain aspects of human behavior, exploring how social anxiety can foster a

DOI: 10.4324/9781003427117-11

psychotic society, sheeple-like behavior, populism, dictatorships, neo-autocratic leadership, and even lead to war. When people experience these regressive behavioral modes, the consequences can be long and lasting. Unfortunately, people often prefer not to think about these aftermaths; however, their tunnel vision prevents them from comprehending that the aftermath can turn out to be more devastating than the storm itself. The process of rebuilding, healing, and reconciliation can take a very long time.

As we have likely experienced firsthand, a good reputation is an incredibly fragile entity. Benjamin Franklin once said, "It takes many good deeds to build a good reputation, and only one bad one to lose it." This holds true not only for an individual's personal reputation but also for a nation. Once again, similar to the aftermath of a storm, managing a reputation can be challenging. We do not always completely understand how it forms, how rapidly it will spread, or what kind of destruction it will cause. The same can be said for maintaining the image of respectable leadership behavior within a country. Reputability, trustworthiness, and dependability are qualities that cannot be developed overnight.

There are many challenges unique to establishing and maintaining a country's leadership reputation or brand image. Due to the psychological impact a reputation can have outside the country's borders, it requires the utmost attention from those living in the country. History has shown that a reassuring leadership reputation can have a ripple effect that positively affects the image of a country, making outsiders aware of a country's capabilities, core values, and contributions to the world at large. A well-articulated leadership brand plays a vital role. It pertains to the country's external reputation and reflects how others view its priorities, commitments, and delivery of promises. It represents what a nation stands for, serving as a basic mission statement. Furthermore, it instills a sense of pride among its citizens, inspiring them to represent their country. When citizens fully commit to their country's leadership brand, they are more likely to advocate for their country and align themselves with its explicit and implicit values. In addition, their civic behavior can serve as a source of inspiration and respect for people from other countries, who will have positive expectations of how they will be treated and the citizens' capabilities. Hence, a country with a highly regarded leadership brand image holds tremendous value for its future.

Quite the opposite is also true: A negative leadership brand can affect how foreigners perceive a specific country to its detriment, impeding its growth and development and instilling little confidence in its willingness to contribute on a global level.

FISH STINK FROM THE HEAD

Reflecting on the examples of leadership given throughout these chapters demonstrates how the behavior of a country's leadership plays a significant role in shaping a country's distinctiveness and identity. The expression "fish stink from the head" is highly appropriate in this context, as the actions and conduct of the leadership at its head greatly determine how it is perceived by outsiders. Every action, decision, and embodiment of a country's leadership has an impact on its brand. As I have emphasized, this negative ripple effect of a leadership brand has been consistently evident in the actions of Putin. It is no exaggeration to say that his "special military operation" has been catastrophic—a poorly thought-out leadership decision. However, due to the relentless propaganda apparatus and media censorship, many Russians still believe the justifications provided by Putin for this war. They don't realize that they're living in an alternative universe. However, those who have access to more accurate news and objective sources of information are experiencing deep embarrassment—shame even—for the actions of their politicians and military. This sense of shame will only be amplified when they travel to other countries and face potentially negative reactions to their nationality. They realize that such horrific behavior by their soldiers implies that their country's leadership has sanctioned it. Unsurprisingly, given the actions of Putin and his inner circle, Russia's leadership brand has been rapidly deteriorating. Many Russians abroad report feeling like outcasts. In fact, in several countries, Russians may no longer be welcomed, a sad example of individuals being punished for the deeds of their dark leaders.

In contrast, when people think of a country like New Zealand, their reactions are notably different. Many will openly appreciate its sense of egalitarianism, the open-mindedness of its people, and the welcoming attitude towards other cultures and nationalities. In addition, people praise its civic culture, the kindness of its citizens, and the way they embrace diversity. It is evident that the former prime minister, Jacinda Ardern, significantly influenced the country's reputation through her behavior, helping to see New Zealand in a very positive light.

By studying the roles played by Putin and Ardern side by side, it is apparent that leaders can have a dramatic influence on the branding of their respective countries. It is clear that a powerful leader like Putin has developed a personal brand that overshadows the original reputation of Russia—a country known for its many eminent scientists, writers, poets, musicians, and other artistic types. Similar negative associations can be made in regard to North Korea, where the "family business," led by Kim Jong Un, has set the prevailing tone. Clearly, the caliber of a country's top leadership can make a substantial difference from a branding perspective.

A SENSE OF OWNERSHIP

It must also be noted that in creating and maintaining a specific leadership brand, even in the presence of toxic leaders, each citizen bears a level of responsibility. They need to continually evaluate whether they're living up to the ideals they associate with their country; whether they like it or not, they too are its representatives. Fulfilling this responsibility, however, necessitates a deeper understanding of the country's leadership brand and the qualities that make it respectable. Only with this knowledge can they act according to what's expected of them. If they don't like what they see, it is their responsibility to take action and change what's happening in their country.

However, changing a country's leadership brand requires a huge amount of effort. In fact, such transformations can take decades or more, as exemplified by post-war Germany. Following World War II, the German people made great efforts to atone for the unfathomable atrocities committed in the past. But they faced the daunting challenge of undoing the damage caused by Hitler's leadership, which saw the burning of books in a land that was once home to many world-renowned philosophers and poets. Subsequently, major re-education efforts were put into action. Yet, it almost seemed that the generation that experienced the atrocities needed to pass away before true reconciliation could be achieved.

This example raises the question of how people in post-Putin Russia will approach the matter. Changing a country's leadership brand is a gradual process that demands energy and commitment towards nurturing its people's mindset, skills, and resources. Essentially, it is about extracting and highlighting the salient aspects of what the country desires to be. Although these activities require a lot of effort, they should be seen as an investment rather than an expense. In the long run, these efforts will undoubtedly prove to be worthwhile, as a strong leadership brand helps a country move forward.

A well-respected leadership brand not only reflects its citizens' deepest values, but it also facilitates individual self-awareness. The deeper the understanding of a nation's leadership brand by its citizens, the better they will understand themselves. They will be more cognizant of their capabilities, their values, and the contributions that they can make in the future. They will also be more prepared to take action when confronted with the forces of individual and collective regression. All in all, a greater degree of self-knowledge will be a means of transcending a dystopian worldview.

BEYOND DYSTOPIA

In the opening chapter, I made reference to the dystopian writings of Franz Kafka. I pointed out how he highlighted the powerlessness of individuals in the face of oppressive and brutal governments. I drew attention to the fact that people living under these regimes were subjected to endless, mindless work, trapped in a world of drudgery. I also noted that feelings of alienation and dehumanization were major themes in his nightmarish works. Sadly, this discussion of a country's leadership brand illustrates how easily it can deteriorate—it takes very little for the world he depicted in fiction to become a chilling reality.

In the various chapters of this book, I have sought to demonstrate how easily our world can assume a dystopian nature. I have observed how quickly individuality can be stifled, how personal freedom can disappear, and how easily we can fall victim to political oppression. With pervasive paranoia, a society can rapidly descend into a living nightmare. The ultimate tragedy of these dystopian worlds is not just the loss of life but also the erosion of individual identities under autocratic regimes. Kafka's tales, like the parable of the boiled frog, serve as a reminder of how easily a population of a country can be oblivious to its subjugation. In this respect, the chapters in this book should be regarded as cautionary tales of how little it takes to precipitate social collapse.

To prevent the descent into dystopia, it is our collective and individual responsibility to avert the manifestation of a Kafkaesque world. With this in mind, I'd like to end this book with the words of the renowned American anthropologist Margaret Mead, who once stated, "Never doubt that a small group of thoughtful, committed individuals can change the world. Indeed, it is the only thing that ever has." In essence, each of us holds the power to shape the world we want to live in.

Index

Printed in the United States
by Baker & Taylor Publisher Services